Evening Standard

Best of...
London

Evening Standard

Best of...
London

Natasha Gilmore

ESB

To Duke

First published in Great Britain in 1996 by
EVENING STANDARD BOOKS
Northcliffe House
2 Derry Street
London W8 5EE

ISBN 1 900625 10 5

Publishing Manager Joanne Bowlby
Editorial Manager Charlotte Coleman-Smith
Production Manager Roger Hall

Designed by Nick Cave

Commissioning Editor for ES Magazine Gaynor Wetherall
With thanks to Brian Matthews

A CIP catalogue record for this book is available from the British Library.

Printed and bound in Great Britain by BPC Hazell Books Ltd, Aylesbury, Bucks.

This book may be ordered by post direct from the publisher,
but please try your bookshop first.

Corporate editions and personal subscriptions of any of the
Evening Standard Guides are available.
Call us for details. Tel 0171 938 6774

Also published in the series:
Children's London (ESB)
The Good Food Shop Guide (ESB)
London Restaurant Guide (Pavilion Books)
London Wine Guide (Pavilion Books)
London Pub Guide (Pavilion Books

Introduction

It is perhaps diversity more than anything else that makes London the greatest capital city in the world. The variety of races, of language and accent, the extraordinary range of buildings and parks and the very different restaurants and bars – Paris, Tokyo and even New York pale by comparison. And, as might be expected in this great city, its services are equally as diverse. There is somebody to dry-clean your socks, pamper your pet and even to protect you from the bogey man. Whatever your needs, London will, by hook or by crook, provide.

Since the *Evening Standard*'s ES magazine became weekly two years ago, it has run a regular column, chronicling the 'Best' of London services. The categories and subjects are as varied as the capital itself. The idea for the column was the brainchild of Stewart Steven, the former Editor of the *Evening Standard*, but it could not have existed without the magazine's tireless Lifestyle Editor, Gaynor Wetherall and her many contributors including: Babara Chandler, Nicole Swingely, Noelle Walsh, Clare Wentworth-Stanley, Denise Elphick, Nancy Patton Wood and Charles Campion. This book is an updated compilation of the best of the 'Best' columns, with many new entries added.

I would particularly like to thank Tamara Wolcough for her tireless research and good humour. Thanks are also due to Kate Sissons and Victoria Coleman-Smith. All information in this book was correct at time of going to press.

NATASHA GILMORE

Airline Caterers

Why is it that whenever you are served a meal on a plane, air turbulence starts with a vengeance and you immediately lose your appetite? I am sure that it's a conspiracy by the pilot and crew, who laugh as everyone turns different shades of green. But then again, what exactly is the amorphous stuff that they expect us to eat? Very often you need to consult the menu to identify the various blobs, snug in their plastic compartment, on the tray in front of you.

Best Afternoon Tea
Caledonian Airlines

Tel (01293) 567 100

Have you ever had an insatiable craving for afternoon tea with all the trimmings as you cruise the skies 37,000 feet above the ground? Caledonian Airlines will not let you down. They offer the whole works: tea, cucumber sandwiches, scones, muffins, cream and jam. All these cholesterol-packed goodies will slip down nicely and give you the sugar rush needed to sustain you for the rest of the flight.

Best Cellar
British Airways Concorde Cellar

Tel (0181) 897 4000

The Concorde cellar is specially selected for British Airways by those in the know and you certainly won't be disappointed by their wines and champagnes as you drink a toast to all things French. Krug, Cuvée Speciale Pommery '81, Veuve Clicquot La Grande Dame '79 or '85 are just some of the bubbly delights on offer. It's just such a pity Concorde flights are so short (but then again, you could always try hiding under the seat to get yourself on to the return trip for more liquid refreshment).

Best for Vegetarians

Air New Zealand

Tel (0181) 846 9595

If you are not a vegetarian, it is almost worth pretending you are, to sample the à la carte menu in Air New Zealand's first class. With three appetisers, five main courses and two desserts to choose from, don't think of the ten-and-a-half-hour flight as a bore but a chance to sample all the yummy food, like mushroom ravioli and warmed banana-and-praline crêpes.

Best Cattle Class

Japan Airlines

Tel (0171) 629 9244

Naturally, most people do not fly economy class but stretch their legs out in front of them in comfort and watch their own video in first class. Wrong! There are more of us crowding into economy class than you realise; we're a friendly bunch (we don't have much choice in the matter), despite the appalling food. Economy-class food is, by reputation, foul, but Japan Airlines will surprise you with Turbot and Scallop Marianne, amongst other delights.

Best for Chef Groupies

Virgin Atlantic Airways

Tel (01293) 562 345

Discovering that a celebrity chef has cooked your supper is the norm in Virgin Upper Class. Relax with the numerous freebies and entertainment they give you while tantalising your tastebuds with a dish prepared by Raymond Blanc himself. You will probably find yourself eyeing the plate of the person sitting next to you for leftovers.

Alterations

There it is in the shop – your dream suit. Beautifully made, right colour, material to die for – the only problem is that the sleeves are down to your ankles and the trousers might as well be shorts. Don't be downhearted. God created the alterations business to take care of these problems.

Best Express Service

Mr Pony

45 Carnaby Street, W1. Tel (0171) 437 9107

These cramped surroundings have housed this Greek-Cypriot tailor for over 20 years. Mr Pony is an institution and has a staff of one – himself. He will alter anything apart from leatherwear and most jobs can be completed within 24 hours. Shirt sleeves are shortened from £8, dresses taken in for £10 and jeans shortened for £5.

Best for Leather and Suede

First Tailored Alterations

85 Lower Sloane Street, SW1. Tel (0171) 730 1400

A staff of eight will perform such miracles as turning a long, lined jacket into a waist-length one. Sheepskins and fake furs are accepted and there is a free quote for those who have an imaginative design idea they want to turn into a reality. Alterations take about a week and skirts and trousers can be shortened from £12–£15.

Best for Simple Jobs

Maurice Alteration Service

5 Monmouth Street, WC2. Tel (0171) 836 9401

For those who want a straightforward, no-nonsense approach. There is one tailor in charge of all alterations and jobs take two to three days to complete. Jackets are taken in from £12, dresses from £6.

Best for Designer Labels

Express Tailoring Services

3 New Burlington Place, W1. Tel (0171) 437 9345

The tailors here are Savile Row-trained and will tackle everything apart from wedding dresses. The team of seven are able, amongst other things, to take the pleats out of skirts and to narrow lapels. Alterations take about a week. Sleeves are shortened for £19.95, trousers taken up for £8.75.

Best for Remodelling

Jeeves

8-10 Pont Street, SW1. Tel (0171) 235 1101

Ever thought of giving your existing wardrobe an overhaul? Here they will convert a day dress into a cocktail dress and taper those hideous flares currently being used as a blanket by your dog. Alterations take from two to ten days. Trousers are shortened from £13, waistbands are replaced for £15.

Alternative Health Therapy

Sometimes that five minutes with your doctor is just not enough. Before you've had a chance to describe your symptoms you are bundled back out of the door with a prescription for a high-level chemical cocktail. Needless to say, a couple of months later you feel just as bad again and you wish that you had taken a different approach. So why not go for the wild and wacky alternative?

Best for Bathtimes

Aquatonics

4 Wellington Close, Ledbury Road, Notting Hill, W11. Tel (0171) 229 1123

Who hasn't spent hours in the bath staring into space and enjoying the cocoon of warm water? Flotation tanks are glorified baths that can help relieve stress and high blood pressure as well as a variety of joint and muscle ailments. At Aquatonics you can float in a tank with a pull-down lid in perfect privacy. For £20 an hour this blissful experience is well worth being shrivelled like a prune for. From Monday–Friday one hour costs £15 before 6pm; £19 evenings and weekends.

Best for Cards

Mysteries

9-11 Monmouth Street, WC2. Tel (0171) 240 3688

Everyone would like to know the answer to certain questions in their life. Health? Happiness? And what about material wealth? A tarot-card reader can help you. At Mysteries, tarot card readers will attempt to divine your future (once you have crossed their palms with £15). They will tell you things about yourself that you thought were secret, and will answer the questions that you 'ask' the cards.

Best for Reducing You to Jelly
London College of Massage

5-6 Newman Passage, W1. Tel (0171) 637 7125

What could be better than closing your eyes and relaxing as someone massages the life into your tired old body? Your first consultation and massage at the London College will cost £40 and subse-
quent sessions will set you back £30 an hour. Alternatively, why not
attend one of their many seminars and courses and learn the skill
yourself? You are sure to make someone very happy.

Best for Reaching for the Stars
The Astrology Shop

78 Neal Street, WC2. Tel (0171) 497 1001.

Here, you and your partner can assess your compatibility rating
using The Astrology Shop's special computerised system. The complex computer programme was years in the making, but you only
have to wait minutes for it to provide you with a character profile or
forecast for the year ahead. For those with wayward children this is
a great opportunity to get a reading which might give you an insight
into their future. Costs are £16 for a character forecast, £18 for a
yearly forecast and £28 for a combination.

Best for Tea Drinkers/Needle Lovers
Chinese Medicine Centre

7 Little Newport Street, WC2. Tel (0171) 287 1095

Almost any ailment can be cured here. Most importantly, you are
treated as an individual and the doctor will make you up a unique
potion of herbs to deal with your particular needs. Acupuncture goes
hand-in-hand with the herbal treatment, so with a combination of
the two you should feel like a new (albeit bruised) person.. Acupun-
ture is £25 including a consultation.

Alternative Sports

If you can't kick a football and your swimming skills only extend as far as doggy-paddle, don't despair – your talents might shine in some of the slightly less conventional sports around. So don't be shy, hunt through your bottom drawer for that old school tracksuit and get moving!

Best for Damon Hill Wannabees
Daytona & Indianapolis Raceways

54 Wood Lane, W12. Tel (0181) 749 2277

If you've ever fancied yourself as a Formula One stud, then this is the place to prove yourself as you race round the track against your opponents. A session on the raceways is the perfect bonding experience for competitive colleagues on an office outing, or, if you are feeling slightly shy, you can take yourself up on the challenge and race against the clock. Pit your skills against the terrifying-sounding Red Eye (10.30pm–1am; £25 per head). The cost of an average session is £25–£42.50 and is well worth the thrill. Once all the excitement is over, you can pause to refuel in the racetrack's American diner.

Best for Knocking Balls

Hurlingham Club

Ranelagh Gardens, SW6. Tel (0171) 736 3148

Some have described discovering croquet as akin to a spiritual awakening. Here at the Hurlingham Club, where the British Open Championships are held every summer, they have the sport down to a fine art. If you prove to be a good sort (and a good shot) they may include you in their club. Ring for membership details.

Best for Night-time Pursuits

National Rivers Authority

Kings Meadow House, Kings Meadow Road, Reading. Tel (01734) 535651

What could be a better alibi than a spot of night fishing? The tranquility of the riverbank will soon help you to forget spoilt children, hysterical spouses and unpaid bills. Imagine it – just you at the water's edge with your fishing rod and a thermos of something warm to keep the chill out. Peace and quiet. Remember a rod licence costs from £1.50–£45, depending on what you want to fish.

Best for the Young at Heart

Skate Attack City Track

Spitalfields Old Market, Brushfield Street, E1. Tel (0171) 267 6961

Unless you are born with your feet already on a board, skateboarding is a notoriously difficult skill to pick up. It's alright when you are small because you don't have so far to fall. Some people, who seem to be clinging to their youth, do brush the dust off their boards and give it a go, but anyone over the age of 17 should probably take a tip and turn to the type of skating you do with two feet instead. Skateboards cost from £39–£360.

Antiquarian Bookshops

Antiquarian bookshops tend to bring images of old-fashioned mustiness to mind. One can almost picture a dimly lit, dusty shop, its owner wearing fraying tweeds and bearing an uncanny resemblance to Anthony Hopkins in that tearjerker of a film, 84 Charing Cross Road. Of course, reality has nothing to do with such romantic notions... or does it?

Best for All-rounders

Henry Pordes Books

58-60 Charing Cross Road, WC2. Tel (0171) 836 9031

This shop has been open for ten years and is distinguished by musty smells and a basement bursting with books. There is always a huge range in stock with good selections on theatre, cinema, and all the performing arts. They also have a small Judeaic section. Prices range from 50p for second-hand paperbacks to £2,000 for rare antiquarian books. There is a ten per cent discount for students. The shop is open from Monday-Friday 10am-7pm

Best for the Big Bad Woolf

Bloomsbury Workshop

12 Galen Place, Off Bury Place, WC1. Tel (0171) 405 0632

This small bookshop, which doubles up as an art gallery, sells all types of work related to the famous Bloomsbury group, as well as first editions, biographies, prints, drawings and paintings. The staff are helpful, and are willing to lend a hand if you cannot track down a certain book. Prices vary from lowish for books and prints to about £6,000 for a quality painting. They also have a mail-order service. Bloomsbury Workshop is open from Monday-Friday 10am-5.30pm.

Best for Boho Intellectuals
Chelsea Rare Books

313 Kings Road, SW3. Tel (0171) 351 0950

Owners Leo and Philippa Bernard have been running this shop since 1973. Specialists in art, architecture, English literature and London history, they have more than 8,000 books with prices ranging from £10 to the high hundreds. There are no fixed discounts but they will try and accommodate those who can't quite make the price. If you venture downstairs you will find a print and watercolour gallery.

Best for Ghostbusting
Maggs Brothers

50 Berkeley Square, W1. Tel (0171) 493 7160

Monday-Friday 9.30-5.00pm

This distinguished premises used to be the Prime Minister's town house and is reputed to be the most haunted property in London. It is run by fourth and fifth generations of the Maggs family, who are the longest occupants in the building. The staff are experts in their own field but if you want their undivided attention, it's best to make an appointment. They specialise in quality collectable books averaging at £100. However, there are some bargains from £5.00

Best for Modern First Editions
Bertram Rota

31 Long Acre (First Floor), WC2. Tel (0171) 836 0723

Monday-Friday 9.30am-5.30pm

Tucked away on the first floor of a large building, this shop is really more of an office. There are between one and two thousand first editions dating from 1890 to the present day, as well as autograph and manuscript material. Prices are high, ranging from £10-£2,000, but they do have exciting finds with many English and American authors.

Antique Dealers

A trip to an antique dealers is like entering a sweet shop. You will be spoilt for choice and undecided on what to buy. Inevitably you will walk away with much more than you intended, but how could you resist that smooth-talking man with all his nice things?

Best for Baubles
S. J. Philips

139 New Bond Street, W1A. Tel (0171) 629 6261

If you are looking for a present which is just that little bit special this is the place to find it. The wonderful people who work here will help you find what you are looking for or let you browse among the many treasures. They specialise in jewellery, snuff boxes and other trinkets. Bring your own trinkets in: they do valuations as well.

Best for Impressive Bits and Pieces
Carlton Hobbs Ltd

46a Pimlico Road, SW1. Tel (0171) 730 3640

At Carlton Hobbs, you will find a hoard of 18th- and 19th-century English and continental furniture which is not to be missed. They often have a wide and impressive selection of Russian furniture which complements the other treasures found in this Aladdin's cave. The staff are very helpful and friendly.

Best for International Treasures

Spink & Son Ltd

5-7 King Street, SW1. Tel (0171) 930 7888

Spink & Son is actually owned by its next-door neighbour, Christie's, but it operates as a totally separate venture. It specialises in a wide range of international delights such as Japanese, Chinese and Indian work and has an impressive collection of coins dating from Greek and Roman times to the present day.

Best for Regal Clientele

Asprey

165-169 New Bond Street, W1. Tel (0171) 493 6767

This is where antique shop meets luxurious mansion. Asprey is impressive in every detail, right down to the doormen. They sell everything here, from tiaras to simple paperweights, and browsing upstairs in the furniture department you could be fooled into thinking you are actually in someone's (very upmarket) house.

Best for TV Personality

John Bly

27 Bury Street, St. James's, SW1. Tel (0171) 930 1292

On Sunday nights John Bly can be seen on our screens in the Antiques Road Show, but you can see him in the flesh if you make a trip to SW1. He specialises in English furniture and works of art and definitely knows his stuff. Why not learn from the man himself and attend one of the seminars that he holds here in the shop? (from £120).

Art Dealers

There is no need to think of art dealers as Lovejoys who get their masterpieces off the back of a lorry. In reality they are legitimate businessmen and women and doing a roaring trade, in spite of the continued gloomy reports of recession and bankruptcy. And art collecting is not just for the rich – many a bargain can be picked up for relatively small amounts of money, so start collecting little by little, make friends with the dealers and before you know it you may have become another budding Saatchi.

Best for Fluttering Hearts

Bill Thomson

Albany Gallery, 1 Bury Street, St. James's, SW1. Tel (0171) 839 6119

Bill Thomson has been in the art dealing business for a number of years and his gallery is small and select. He has been described as 'very British' and in the 1960s he was considered to be quite a dish. Even today, eyes often light up at the mention of his name. Thomson specialises in British watercolours and his client list is wide.

Best for a High Profile

Johnny van Haeften Ltd

13 Duke Street, SW1. Tel (0171) 930 3062

Johnny van Haeften used to work at Christie's but has since branched out on his own. He now deals in Dutch and Flemish Old Masters. He attends all the shows making sure that his presence is known, and is a likeable man always on hand to please the customer. Consequently, he has a very good client base of trusting and loyal customers.

Best for Knowing What He Likes

Michael Pruskin Gallery

73 Kensington Church Street, W8 Tel: (0171) 937 1994

Michael Pruskin specialises in Art Nouveau and Art Deco and is interested in 20th-century art and design. His worldwide clientele trust his keen eye. Pruskin may be a softly-spoken man but that should not fool you; he knows exactly what he wants and what is best for his clients.

Best for Success

Richard Green (Fine Paintings)

39 and 44 Dover Street, W1
4 and 33 New Bond Street, W1. Tel (0171) 493 3939

Successful art dealer Richard Green has a very commanding presence and can only be described as larger than life. He runs four different art galleries in London and all of them are doing booming business. His galleries on Dover Street hold 17th- to 19th- century paintings while the New Bond Street branches concentrate on modern British works.

Best for Victorian Paintings

Christopher Wood Ltd

141 New Bond Street, W1. Tel (0171) 499 7411

Christopher Wood is yet another art dealer who used to work at Christie's but has since branched out on his own. He now runs a successful business which specialises in Victorian and pre-Raphaelite paintings. Christopher has a good client list and is thoroughly likeable and helpful. When he is not running his busy gallery he spends his time writing books.

Art Galleries

Wandering through an art gallery trying to interpret blobs of paint on the canvases while eating papery morsels masquerading as crisps and sipping sparkling white wine is, unbelievably, seen as an enjoyable social event by some. The irony is that with all the pretentious waffle and air-kissing going on, you risk missing a genuine masterpiece hanging on the wall. My tip is to skip the opening and avoid the simpering idiots. Instead, arrive during the daytime and contemplate your favourite picture in peace and quiet.

Best Alternative Art
Alternative Art Galleries
c/o 47a Brushfield Street, E1. Tel (0171) 375 0441

Alternative Art Galleries are a collection of empty shops that exhibit the works of lesser-known artists. The work is varied, ranging from sculptures to oil paintings, with prices from £20 to £1,000 (average £300). The shops are all in the W1 area and are scattered along Chiltern Street and Marylebone High Street. Trading laws make it illegal to buy the art on the shop premises so it's a case of writing a hasty cheque at the side of the road.

Best for Novice Collectors
The Cut Gallery
82 The Cut, SE1. Tel (0171) 207 8388

A fairly recent addition to the London art scene, this gallery has been open for nearly two years. The works, by undergraduates from the southern art region, have been selected by editors of various art publications and can be picked up for about £50 which is ideal if you are buying art for the first time. You can also view work by more established artists such as Peter Nevin and Frank Bowlin.

Best Sculpture and Graphics
Curwen Gallery

4 Windmill Street, W1. Tel (0171) 636 1459

The Curwen Gallery has an annual exhibition programme which includes group and individual shows where contemporary British and international paintings, sculptures and graphics are exhibited. The works vary in price, but quite a few can be bought for less than £500.

Best for Young Black Artists
196 Gallery

194-198 Railton Road, SE24. Tel (0171) 978 8309

This gallery holds new and exciting works of art costing between £100 and £1,500. The focus of the gallery is on two- and three-dimensional work by young black artists, although art and craft from all over the world is also exhibited.

Best for Young Contemporaries
Cadogan Contemporary

108 Draycott Avenue, SW3. Tel (0171) 581 5451

They hold 22 exhibitions a year here, featuring work by established artists as well as recent graduates. The paintings are mostly figurative and the gallery holds a large stock of work by various gallery artists for viewing. Artists who have exhibited here include Catherine Goodman, Sargy Mann and Emma McLure.

Au Pairs

To au pair or to full-time-nanny it? This is the perennial middle-class working mother's dilemma. Some full-time working parents cannot abide the thought of, or have no room for, another person in the house so will farm out their children to all-day, all-year-round nurseries. Au pairs are undoubtedly the cheaper option. Home Office regulations require that au pairs are single, between the ages of 17 and 27, and are given their own room and pocket money along with free time to study. Prices vary vastly and good agencies will sort out any teething troubles and refunds if things don't work out. Many agencies carry an FRES (Federation of Recruitment and Employment Services) employment licence.

Best International Agency

Au Pair International

14 Gloucester Road, SW7. Tel (0171) 225 0067

This well-established agency in central London draws the majority of its au pairs from Germany, as these frauleins have gained a good reputation for their efficiency and down-to-earth approach. However, hot on the their heels in the popularity stakes are Finnish, South African, Icelandic, French and Swedish girls. Au Pair International prides itself on looking after the welfare of its charges and they are genuinely interested in the girls' well-being, which takes some of the strain off the family when Helga is found weeping into her pillow every night. The agency organises an au-pair club which meets twice a month and where the girls can socialise with each other and organise day trips around England or weekends in Paris or Amsterdam. This agency is, apparently, popular with celebrity parents. Rates are £75 plus VAT for placements of up to three months; £150 plus VAT for six months; £200 plus VAT for twelve months. There is no charge for replacement during the first month.

Best for Antipodeans
Koala Nannies

22 Craven Terrace, W2. Tel (0171) 404 4224

Not, strictly speaking, an au-pair agency, Koala Nannies will help you find a reliable, efficient extra pair of hands whether you require a full-time nanny or a not-so-expensive mother's help. The popularity of antipodean girls is growing as they tend to be very good at mucking in and don't baulk at extra duties. Agency boss Catherine Mansel-Lewis makes frequent trips to Australia and New Zealand where she personally interviews prospective workers. The agency has recently introduced the Koala Club, which offers discounts in many different consumer outlets including restaurants, hairdressers, boutiques and children's shops. Rates work out at one month of the nanny's salary.

Best for Male Au Pairs
Family Friend

16 Millers Court, Chiswick Mall, W4. Tel (0181) 563 0604

The demand for male au pairs is increasing daily according to Marilyn Schroeder, who teamed up with her own Bosnian home help to bring the first male au pairs over to Britain. Although the agency deals with male and female au pairs from all over Europe she finds those from Bosnia and Herzegovina the most reliable. Agencies abroad interview the prospective au pairs and Marilyn then passes the information on to interested families in the UK. When a suitable au pair is found the family will meet him or her at the airport together with a company representative who will help to put everyone at their ease. The fee for a long-term placement (upwards of three months) is £159, while the short-term fee is £45. Should your au pair leave within the first four weeks you can claim a refund of 50 per cent (this applies to long-term placements only).

Auction Houses

Most people run through auction rooms with their arms firmly by their sides, their twitch under control and not daring to blink just in case they mistakenly acquire something they don't have a hope in hell of ever affording. Trust me, take it slow and look around; you will be surprised by what you find and, once you are accustomed to the ways of the auction world, you will be able to twitch all you like.

Best for Decorating First Flats
Lots Road Galleries

71-74 Lots Road, SW10. Tel (0171) 351 7771

This is ideal for newly married couples short on cash. There are many bargains to be found and the Sunday viewing hours make it possible to take things at a relaxed rate, so there'll be no fraught arguments as you browse around the auction items at your leisure. The only quibbles might come when you realise that your tastes are very different and you are not suited to live under the same roof...

Best for Regional Road Shows
Christie's, South Kensington

85 Old Brompton Road, SW7. Tel (0171) 581 7611

Christie's South Kensington handles a broad range of goods, from paintings, ceramics, jewellery and books to pop and film memorabilia. Prices are not as astronomical as those at the main branch in Kings Street, so you can expect to find a few bargains here. The regional road shows that they organise throughout the year are not to be missed.

Best for Jewellery

Hatton Garden Auction

70 Hatton Garden, EC1. Tel (0171) 242 6452

If you are in this area at lunch time Hatton Garden Auction is not to be missed. Feeling rather like a small club, it's intimate, friendly and charged with energy as people rush in during their lunch breaks to buy the jewellery sold by auction. You can find both modern and antique pieces for unbelievably good prices.

Best for Variety

Sotheby's

34-35 New Bond Street, W1. Tel (0171) 493 8080

Sotheby's has been around for over 250 years and has expanded all over the world – a branch of Sotheby's is now almost as common a sight abroad as a Visa machine. The list of things that you can find here is vast. After one visit, you could be the proud owner of anything from an old master to a modern-day guitar.

Barbers

Men like to be pampered just as much as women, and a trip to the barber to be shaved and shorn is a time to relax. You won't find any of the girly decor of your average hairdressing salon here; just the comforting smells of leather and lotions and the constant sound of snipping scissors.

Best Central Location

Jack's

The Basement, 25a Old Compton Street, W1. Tel (0171) 734 2954

This barber's shop has a genuinely old-fashioned feel to it. It is owned by Jack 'the Clipper', who lives up to his name by being a whizz with the clippers. His clientele pay £20 for a haircut. There are five swivel chairs.

Best for Dandies

G.F. Trumper

9 Curzon Street, W1. Tel (0171) 499 1850
20 Jermyn Street, SW1. Tel (0171) 734 1370
Simpson, Piccadilly, W1. Tel (0171) 734 2002, ext 342

This chain of barber shops offers the ultimate grooming experience. Stepping into one of their shops is like walking into another time and they have many own-brand lotions and creams on hand to buy. Prices are £13.50 for a cut and £19.50 for a cut and shampoo.

Best for Footie Fans

Gino's

33A Dean Street, W1. Tel (0171) 437 2029

This 1950s-style Soho haunt is a favourite for soccer fans who can talk strategies with the football-mad staff. One of their star clients is Gerard Depardieu, who refuses to trust anyone else to cut his hair.

While you are being groomed you can enjoy a cappuccino or an espresso. A wash and cut costs £14.50.

Best for Style
Vidal Sassoon Barber Shop
56 Brook Street, W1. Tel (0171) 493 5428

Celebrities such as Bryan Ferry and Mel Gibson have had their hair cut here by graduates of the Sassoon barber-training course. The décor is no-nonsense wood panelling with traditional barber's-shop chairs. Prices for a wash and cut range from £34.50–£50.

Best for Tradition
Austin Reed
103-113 Regents Street, W1. Tel (0171) 734 6789

This establishment opened in 1930 and can boast many esteemed gentlemen and politicians amongst its clientele. On entering, you'll be greeted by the sight of nine swivel chairs and an interior that seems not to have changed at all over the years. The only services which, sadly, are not available, are baths and showers for the busy English gent. A wash and cut will cost you £14.

Best Value
Dino's
16 Jerdan Place, SW6. Tel (0171) 381 1144

The barbers here will not only give you a great haircut (without a wash) for only £5.20 but are perfectly amenable to shaving 'Chelsea' across the back of the heads of football fanatics. The nearby football ground means there is a steady stream of people filling the nine chairs and the lively atmosphere is kept up by the constant banter of the Cypriot, Italian and Turkish barbers.

Bed Shops

We spend a third of our lives in them, but most of our beds are over ten years old. Essential for proper rest, relaxation and so on, choosing a bed is one of the most crucial decisions you can make, on a par with choosing a car. By the way, a firm mattress is not necessarily better for posture, contrary to popular belief.

Best for Antique Wood
Simon Horn

117-121 Wandsworth Bridge Road, SW6. Tel (0171) 731 1279
Fourth floor, Harvey Nichols, Knightsbridge, SW1. Tel (0171) 235 5000

Simon Horn started his business in 1982 and is already considered Europe's leading expert in wooden beds. He is obsessed with finding new models, both here and abroad. His famed 'Lit Bâteau', widely copied elsewhere, has 18 different interpretations. He uses solid beech, rosewood, walnut or wild-cherry wood. Prices range from £700 to £5,335 for a large king-sized bed in solid rosewood.

Best for Pine
Litvinoff and Fawcett

238 Gray's Inn Road, WC1. Tel (0171) 278 5391
9 Chalk Farm Road, NW1. Tel (0171) 482 0066
281 Hackney Road, E2. Tel (0171) 739 3480

Julian Litvinoff uses Baltic pine from renewable forests in Russia and Scandinavia to make his beds. A 5ft-wide bed, with do-it-yourself screw-in slats, costs £78. Turned legs, panels, headboards and drawers are also available. A beautifully designed sleigh bed, traditionally jointed, costs £495. Contract-quality mattresses cost from £128 for the 5ft-wide model.

Best in the West End

Capital Dreams

180 Tottenham Court Road, W1. Tel (0171) 323 1066

There are two floors here, packed with over 100 beds and 150 mattresses. All beds are guaranteed for ten years, and it is possible to test the suitability of any bed at home for 28 days. If you are still not happy with your choice you can exchange it at any branch of Capital Dreams, and if you can find their beds cheaper anywhere else, they will refund double the difference. Prices range from £99 for a single bed to £149 for a double.

Best for Waterbeds

The London Waterbed Company

99 Crawford Street, W1. Tel (0171) 935 1111

Ingrid Layton and Maureen Pope have been selling a wide variety of waterbeds for eight years. 'Softside' models resemble ordinary beds and come in conventional sizes. 'Hardside' waterbeds, cradled in a wooden frame, come in a variety of finishes and are 7ft long. There is a choice of four mattress options: free flotation (a gentle rocking movement), semi-waveless (this stabilises within six seconds), motionless (stabilises within two to three seconds) and super-motionless (stabilises within a second). All models require a heater which is separated from the water mattress by a safety lining. The shop will arrange professional installation, which includes filling the bed by means of a hose. Single beds start at around £395 inclusive.

Bloody Marys

Many an undignified argument has been fought over what goes into the making of a perfect Bloody Mary. Sherry or no sherry? Celery salt or horseradish? Clamato or tomato or both? Real Russian vodka or plain old Smirnoff? Worcestershire sauce and Tabasco or both? Whatever the ingredients, there is no disputing the fact that whatever happened the night before, a first-class Bloody Mary can set you straight the day after.

Best for Brunch

Christopher's

18 Wellington Street, WC2. Tel (0171) 240 4222

Davis Marazzi, the head barman at this American-inspired establishment, is fast gaining a reputation for concocting the best hangover cure in London. His Bloody Marys include extra Worcestershire sauce and lime rather than lemon juice. He also recommends his own variation, which he calls 'Bloody Marazzi' (a basic Bloody Mary garnished with a Mozzarella ball, a baby tomato and a slice of avocado). After one of these creations, you won't be needing lunch. Cost: £5.50.

Best for a Classic

The Library Bar at The Lanesborough Hotel

1 Lanesborough Place, SW1. Tel (0171) 259 5599

Laurent, the barman, is a strict traditionalist and insists that any deviation from the classic recipe is not a Bloody Mary. So for the record, here is his definitive recipe: 1 quarter vodka (anything but Stolly, as it is too strong), 2cm lemon juice, a dash of Tabasco, 2cm Worcestershire sauce, celery salt, tomato juice (not the fresh kind – it's too liquid), pepper, a celery stalk and lime wedge to garnish. Cost: £7

Best for Prizes
The American Bar at the Savoy

The Savoy Hotel, The Strand, WC2. Tel (0171) 836 4343

The assistant head barman, Salim Khouri, has been with this establishment for 27 years and recently won an award for the most delectable Bloody Mary in London. His secret, he reckons, is freshly-squeezed tomato juice; however, he's not a stickler and will cater for individual tastes and fads. Cost: £6.75

Best for Sundays
The Grenadier

18 Wilton Row, SW1. Tel (0171) 235 3077

This quintessential British pub is what the Yanks no doubt imagine all our alehouses to look like. The Bloody Marys here are so popular on Sundays that a special bar has been set up for them. You purchase your ticket at the main bar and wait for the barman, Paul Gibb, to work his magic. The base is quite straightforward: vodka, tomato juice, etc., but the secret ingredient – a blend of three types of alcohol – remains just that. The concoction is mixed in a cocktail shaker for a full minute, producing a frothy effect. Cost: £4

Best for Spice
Kensington Place Restaurant and Bar

205 Kensington Church Street, W8. Tel (0171) 727 3184

Renowned throughout West London for his fiery Bloody Marys, Chin, the barman at this trendy dive, has set many a hangover straight with his miraculous concoction. His approach is fairly straightforward: 1 large measure of vodka, 1 dash of dry sherry, a smidgen of lemon juice, salt, pepper, celery salt, chilli-ketchup, tomato juice and, the *pièce de résistance*, grated horseradish, all vigorously shaken and poured over ice.... to die for at £5.

Boarding Kennels

The welfare of your dog or cat is of utmost importance when you are sampling the sand, sea and sangria or just paying a duty call to the in-laws. It's difficult to have a happy holiday if you are worrying about your furry friend. Seek out one of the boarding kennels listed here and worry no more.

Best for Medical Attention
Chingford Boarding, Quarantine Kennels and Cattery
160 Chingford Mount Road, E4. Tel (0181) 529 0979

With a veterinary practice on site, these kennels have immediate access to one vet for animals in quarantine and another for boarders. Dogs are exercised up to six times a day. Cats have outdoor individual runs and the sleeping quarters are large, with plastic baskets and infrared heating. Collection and delivery are easily arranged and quirky diets are catered for. Prices: dogs from £5.95 per day in high season (July to September), cats £4.85 per day in high season. Vet insurance is £2.50, bathing costs £5.

Best for Gatwick
Ifield Park Cattery and Kennels
Bonnets Lane, Ifield, Crawley, Sussex. Tel (01293) 537 345

The recently demolished cattery has been replaced with a deluxe version, a double-glazed, heated affair with deep cavities for sleeping and long runs for exercise. All the pets' details are logged into a computer for quick reference. Dogs are exercised daily under supervision and the rest of their day is spent in roomy runs. Animals that stay longer than four days merit a bath and all are groomed before going home. Prices: dogs from £6 per day plus VAT, cats from £3.50 per day.

Best for Heathrow

Silverdale Kennels and Cattery

Bedfont Road, Feltham, Middx. Tel (0181) 890 1784

Just ten minutes from Heathrow, these kennels take both cats and dogs and manageress Maggie Embleton will ensure that your animal is returned to you in the same condition you left it. All dogs have an 8ft x 4ft heated kennel and are given a minimum of four half-hourly walks a day (or more if you request it). Cats have indoor accommodation leading on to a 7ft run. Inoculated animals only. Prices: £8 per day for dogs, £4.50 for cats.

Best for Views

Way Farm Kennels and Cattery

Guildford Road, Ottershaw, Surrey. Tel (01932) 873 239

Set in 50 acres of farmland complete with a five-acre wood, fields and pastures, these kennels are very picturesque. Karina Le Mare has run the establishment for the past 18 years. Dogs are pampered with their own 60ft run, and sleeping quarters vary in size but all are up to an excellent standard. Cats can climb tree trunks in their own roomy runs. Faddy diets are catered for and inoculations must be up to date. Collection and delivery can be arranged for anywhere in London. Prices: dogs from £5.50 per day plus VAT, cats from £4.25 per day plus VAT.

Bodyguards

Ever since THAT film starring Kevin Costner and Whitney Houston came out the bodyguarding industry in England has boomed — for every job available there are 50 to 60 applicants. The best recognised course is run by the British International Bodyguard Association and only one woman to date has passed. So if you are a huge international star or maybe you just fancy a bit of an ego trip, why not hire one for the day?

Best-looking

ICP

Victoria House, 98 Victoria Street, SW1. Tel (0171) 915 0054

Twenty-nine-year-old owner, William Geddes, is ex-public school, ex-army and a real charmer. He is so courteous and polite that it's hard to imagine the steel that lurks beneath the smooth exterior. His firm specialises in looking after wealthy high-profile businessmen who come from overseas and feel the need for protection when in England. Prices range from £200–£1,000 per day.

Best for Showbiz

Showsec

23a Benell Road, N7. Tel (0171) 609 9411

This organisation has become the ultimate bodyguard firm on the celebrity circuit. George Michael used them to ward off unwelcome attention during his famous Sony trial, and Barbara Streisand and Mick Hucknall also rely on their services when in town. Mick Upton, head of the company, is keen to dispel the myth that bodyguards have to be over six foot and weighing 20 stone with little brain matter. "At the moment you need absolutely no qualifications to look after a star, but the job does require a high degree of training if it is to be done well", he says.

Best for Status Symbols
Ivor Spencer School For Butlers

12 Little Bones, SE21. Tel (0181) 670 5585/8424

Although this company is best known for providing butlers and toastmasters there is an increasing demand for British-Butlers-cum-Bodyguards, especially from soap stars in California. Spencer's Specials, as they are known, are trained by ex-SAS personnel and are taught to shoot to kill. They usually earn about £15,000 per year, but in America their salaries can be as high as $60,000. One recent protégé turned down $40,000 a year plus perks because he was expected to dress up in a pink uniform with matching patent pumps!

Best for Taking Abroad
Control Risks

83 Victoria Street, SW1. Tel (0171) 222 1552

If you are very important and are doing business abroad in dodgy areas these are probably the guys for you. Top of the danger list at present are Algiers, Sierra Leone, Karachi, Pakistan and parts of Russia. Control Risks have a pool of around 50 ex-military personnel who will ease your path. Bodyguards from this company cost from about £400 per day plus expenses.

Best for Visiting Arabs
Crown Protection Services

83 Priory Road, NW6. Tel (0171) 328 3000

Amongst the numerous security services this company offers, including royal bomb sweeps, its most popular request is providing protection for visiting Arabs and their families. Although it sounds reasonable enough at £25 per hour, the cost soon mounts up if wives, chidren and accompanying entourage require 24-hour protection as well. They provide excellent protection when shopping.

Bookshops

There is nothing so frustrating as going to a bookshop with a specific title in mind only to find that the huge one on your local high street doesn't have it in stock. Buying a book in London can be a hugely gratifying experience if you know which shops to go to.

Best Children's Bookshop

Puffin Children's Bookshop

1 The Market, Covent Garden, WC2. Tel (0171) 416 3000

Cute duck footprints will lead baby boffins around this Child-friendly shop which delights in a Beatrix Potter Room, a reading corner and just about every children's adventure story known to man. The vast array of books caters for ages ranging from newborns to teenagers.

Best Crime Bookshop

Murder One

71-73 Charing Cross Road, WC2. Tel (0171) 734 3483

Every aspect of crime from murders to muggings can be found at this down-to-earth, no-frills-attached shop. Sherlock Holmes fans will delight in the entire section devoted to their hero. If your tastes are more geared to real-life murders and mysteries there are many modern titles featuring the dastardly deeds of Lord Lucan, the Kray twins, Myra Hindley et all.

Best Foodie Bookshop

Books For Cooks

4 Blenheim Crescent, London W11. Tel (0171) 221 1992

Set in the heart of trendy Notting Hill, this wonderful shop is a solid fixture in transient surroundings. The foodie manuals come from all over the world and everything you have ever wanted to know about any aspect of grub can be found here. An added bonus is the café at the back of the shop which sells simple scoff at good prices.

Best for Sci-Fi

Forbidden Planet

71 New Oxford Street, W1. Tel (0171) 497 2150

This shop enjoys a cult following. It is the sort of place frequented by eternal students and ageing radio presenters and holds a truly impressive stock of vintage comics, fanzines, books, videos, etc, which all pay tribute to classic heroes like Spiderman, Thunderbirds and Batman. There is also a model department which allows you to build your own creations from such cult classics as Dr Who and Star Trek.

Best Travel Books

The Travel Bookshop

13 Blenheim Crescent, W11. Tel (0171) 229 5260

An excellent bookshop for seasoned or aspiring travellers, or the merely curious. The staff are very clued up and will happily answer any questions. The huge selection of books range from beautifully produced photo-journals to antiquarian editions of Robinson Crusoe.

Chauffeur-driven Cars

It's Saturday afternoon and there is not a single parking space anywhere near your favourite shop. Sounds familiar? Well, there is a solution to this problem: a chauffeur-driven car. It may sound impossibly flashy and monstrously expensive but if you club together with friends it is not as pricey as you might think – just think of envious glances you will attract.

Best for the Airport
Mayfair Carriages

8 Chancel Street, Blackfriars, SE1. Tel (0171) 383 5588

Reaching the airport in time for your flight, feeling cool, calm and relaxed and without losing your luggage or children on the way, can seem impossible at times. Ride with this firm and you will be truly pampered with a fully stocked bar, telephone, TV with video, tinted windows for complete privacy and a uniformed chauffeur. The trip will set you back £80 for Heathrow and £120 for Gatwick. The cars fit up to seven people and can also be hired for shopping trips for a minimum of three hours.

Best for Christmas Shopping
Location Chauffeurs

34 Kingshead Hill, E4. Tel (0181) 524 1169

Shop all day long with a helpful chauffeur who knows the best places to take you and will even carry your bags for you. The car is a Mercedes 'S'-class and for eight hours, or covering forty miles, this service will cost you £185 plus VAT. Shop till you drop!

Most Discreet

Hylax Luxury Car Service

82 Darwin Court, Gloucester Avenue, NW3. Tel (0171) 911 0570

If you are not into being flash and are just interested in getting from A to B in comfort then this is the company for you. The cars are either Volvo 760 GLEs or 960 24v saloons. The chauffeur is uniformed and the car is packed with airline information, telephones and that essential item for travelling round London: an umbrella. Price £12 per hour, £10 per hour for waiting time.

Best for Glamour

Camelot Cars

Headfort Place, SW1. Tel (0171) 235 0234

If a person's name has been up in lights you can bet they have been in one of Camelot's cars. Chauffeurs have been trained in all areas, including first aid and anti-ambush techniques. To go on a daytime shopping trip in a Mercedes SEL will cost you £28 per hour; expect to pay £45 per hour, including VAT, for hitting the town at night in a Silver Shadow. Their cars are flash to look at and range from a Scorpio to a Rolls-Royce.

Best for Security

Limousines of London

Milton House, 2 Fernshaw Road, SW10. Tel (0171) 351 7408

Anyone who feels the need to be protected should make this their first choice. As well as a chauffeur-driven car you can also hire a bodyguard and a translator at an extra cost. There is a wide range of cars, including a Rolls-Royce Silver Shadow costing £140 for four hours or 30 miles' travel. If that is beyond your budget a more modest Daimler Sovereign saloon costs just £25 per hour.

Chimney Sweeps

I am afraid it's time to dispel the myth that all chimney sweeps are just like the ones in Mary Poppins: all-singing and all-dancing. Happily, neither do they leave little boys stuck in chimneys as they did in years gone by. So how does the modern chimney sweep operate?

Best for Hidden Secrets

B.G. Wright

11 Harvill Road, North Cray, Sidcup, Kent.
Tel (0181) 302 5468

What do you think people leave up their chimneys? Mr Glyn of B.G. Wright has found unopened letters to Father Christmas dating from more than 40 years ago as well as love letters hidden by an adulterous wife. And they don't just discover secrets: Mr Glyn also rescued two baby squirrels last year which he has appropriately named Sooty and Sweep. Prices: £29.50, not including VAT, for a small house, otherwise £10 per floor.

Best for Old and New

Willis Chimney Sweeps

62 Attlee Road, Hayes, Middlesex. Tel (0181) 841 8718

Nigel Willis inherited Willis Chimney Sweeps in 1981 from a 72-year-old sweep and now carries on the business with unfailing enthusiasm. He has brought together the old and the new by keeping the traditional sweep's brushes but investing in modern accessories. He even has a dry-ice machine to test for leaks. He cleans chimneys dressed in white gloves, dark trousers and a cotton shirt. Prices from £26.

Best for Original Vehicle
Clean Sweep

115a Downs Court Road, Purley, Surrey. Tel (0181) 763 1087

Chris Blackman is keen to let the world know that not all sweeps are covered in soot 24 hours a day. Apparently, having cleaned out an inglenook in a pub you are not going to be acceptable at a house with a white carpet until you have had a good scrub up. Blackman motors from job to job in his pride and joy – a 1961 juniper-over-pine Rover with his name on the side and a rather creative sign featuring a sweep's brushes adorning the top. Prices from £18.

Best for Tradition
Andre Dupré

7 Carrington Gardens, E7. Tel (0181) 519 0600

Andre Dupré left South Africa for London's East End in 1946, where he set up his business. Gone are the days when he used to ride around on a bicycle come rain or shine, but he still has some incredible stories to tell. For £40, André will give your chimney a thorough sweep, a safety and smoke test and a certificate.

Best for Weddings
Milbarrow's (incorporating Bliss Bros.)

Parkfield Farmhouse, Hophurst Lane, Crawley Down, West Sussex.
Tel (0181) 657 7081/3006

Apart from being one of the biggest chimney sweeping firms in the London area, with a fleet of six vans, Milbarrow's also hire their sweeps out for weddings. Apparently it was a Victorian custom to invite a sweep and his black cat to stand outside the church in hat and coat-tails and be the first person the bride saw as a married woman. What that has to do with cleaning chimneys is beyond me, but it seems like a lucrative sideline. Prices from £20.

Cinema Bars

There is nothing better than a good film for a quick fix of metro escapism, but I bet not many of you think of stopping off for a quick pint in a cinema bar before heading for a film. Most filmgoers are too busy fighting their way to the front of the queue for ice-cream and Coke. Why not relax, take it easy and sit in the bar laughing at the poor idiots spilling their popcorn at the refreshment counter?

Best for Italian Food

ICA

12 Carlton House Terrace, SW1, Tel (0171) 930 0493

The ICA have recently embarked on a huge refurbishment for their café. It used to sport the minimalist look but now it is splashed with colour and is ultra-modern. People are drawn to this inviting place and sit transfixed by the loud and garish colours. By the way, you don't have to just sit and look – they have yummy Italian food on sale after 9pm and a variety of snacks beforehand. The bar is licensed from 12am–3pm and from 5.30pm to midnight, so if the film leaves you a little shaky, you have time to recover with a drink.

Best for Optics

The Metro

11 Rupert Street, W1. Tel (0171) 437 0757

This bar is the social meeting point for the cinema. Candy-stripes line the walls with pretty mirrored glass shelves. You can munch on coffee-and-walnut cake and choose between a Grolsch or – for teetotallers – an Aqua Libra. Unfortunately it's closed till September 1996 for refurbishing but will open with films celebrating the seventh Latin American Film Festival.

Best for Retro Style

Rio

107 Kingsland High Street, E8. Tel (0171) 254 6677

This cinema is one of the oldest in London and prides itself on its history. Restoration and renovations have taken place and the old sandwich bar is now a 1930s-style café decorated in black and white. They are not licensed here so you can't sink a few beers, but you can indulge yourself on home-made cakes, Loseley ice-cream and fresh filtered coffee.

Best for Stills

National Film Theatre

South Bank, SE1. Tel (0171) 928 3232

You won't find the usual 1970s cinema décor of brown and orange here, but stylish black and cream with black-and-white stills of drinking scenes on the walls. On a Friday night a pianist will tinkle away on the ivories and you can listen in comfort while sipping one of a variety of bottled beers, including Red Stripe and Carlsberg.

Best for View

Minema

43 Knightsbridge, SW1. Tel (0171) 823 1269

People can sit and have a meal in this small café next-door to an equally small cinema. Great for those London nights when you don't want to venture too far out into the cold and you need your whole evening's entertainment within close quarters. The food is superb and consists of basics such as pasta, or chicken with new potatoes. Pose by the window which looks out on to Hyde Park or stand by the licensed bar and look over the people who had the same idea as you.

Cobblers

"Cobbler, cobbler, mend my shoe, make it ready by half past two," — *so the nursery rhyme goes, but for lucky Londoners, fiction becomes fact. Like Imelda Marcos you may have more than 100 pairs of shoes in your wardrobe but there's only one pair that make your feet sing. They are also the pair that are constantly falling apart, but will you part with them? No way! So thank heaven for cobblers, who will spend hours painstakingly gluing and nailing to bring your much-loved shoes back to life.*

Best for Oddballs

Feet First

26 St Peter's Street, Soho, W1. Tel (0171) 734 0417

Unusual requests are the norm here. Partner Chris Christoforou did not bat an eyelid when a transvestite came in to ask if the tops of a pair of women's thigh-high boots could be widened. Theatre shoes keep them busy but they are able to cope with all requests, no matter how weird and wonderful. They will fix your shoes the same day if possible. Men's heels cost from £4.95 while women's heels cost £2.45.

Best for Old Stagers

Farey & Sons

37 The Cut, Blackfriars, Southwark, SE1. Tel (0171) 928 5352

This business was established in 1928 by the father of the current proprietors, Charles and Derek. Today, the brothers deal with all kinds of shoes. The oldest pair that they have worked their magic on is a pair of early 1960s lace-ups. What may surprise people is that they also repair trainers with just the same dedication. Shoes can take up to two days to repair and men's heel repairs cost £4.70, women's from £2.20 to £2.80.

Best for Roller Skates
Mayfair Cobblers
4 Whitehouse Street, W1. Tel (0171) 491 3426

Footwear, no matter what sort, is a passion at Mayfair Cobblers. Tap shoes, mountain boots, leather slippers... the Starlight Express performers even have their rollerskates mended here. The time it takes depends on the job but most repairs can be done in a day. Men's heel repairs cost £5.95 and women's heels are £2.85.

Best for Thoroughbreds
The Complete Cobbler
28 Tottenham Street, W1 & 253 Eversholt Street, NW1. Tel (0171) 636 9040

George Zorlakkis used to be a shoemaker by trade so he knows more about footwear than most. He specialises in trade repairs for Timberland, Kurt Geiger and Gucci, amongst others. You can wait for your repairs or pick them up at the end of the day. Men's rubber heels cost £6.50, women's £2.80.

Comedy Clubs

Have you ever noticed that no one smiles on the streets of London? And who would dare to utter a giggle while travelling on the Underground? Everyone looks like they have just lost their job or there has been a death in the family. There seems to be a serious sense-of-humour failure going on, but there is one way of escaping all this doom and gloom — try one of the many comedy clubs that are dotted around London. Go on, give it a bash — smiling won't kill you and you will only get more wrinkles if you keep on frowning.

Best for Cheap Laughs

Red Rose Cabaret

129 Seven Sisters Road, N7. Tel (0171) 281 3051

Entertainment-wise, this club and its acts are as good as or better than any of the better-known London comedy clubs around. But what really makes this place stand out is the entrance fee, which is dirt cheap for the great evening out that you will inevitably have. Place yourself at one of the long raised tables, drink the bargain basement alcohol and sit back and enjoy yourself.

Best for Credibility

The Comedy Store

1 Oxenden Street, SW1. Tel (01426) 914 433

The Comedy Store is probably the most famous alternative comedy venue in the country. It is always filled to the brim at weekends, so it is probably advisable to try to squeeze in here on a Thursday night in order to avoid the crowds. The Comedy Store Players are always on good form and can make even the most miserable sod smile. Improvised comedy can be seen on Wednesdays and Sundays.

Best for Good Behaviour and Oriental Food

Jongleurs

49 Lavender Gardens, SW11; also Middle Yard, Camden Lock, Chalk Farm Road, N1. Tel 0171 924 2766

Probably the best-known comedy store in Great Britain, Jongleurs has been going for over 10 years now. There are two venues, one in Clapham and the other in trendy Camden. Well-known stand-up comics spawned by this establishment include Tim Clark and Phil Jupitus. Along with the excellent acts, good food with an oriental slant is also available and comes in bamboo steamer baskets at a reasonable price. Membership costs £5 per year and groups should book. However, single sex parties, beware − a good behaviour bond has to be made and paid in advance. The amount is solely at the discretion of the management and redeemable only if you mind your Ps and Qs.

Best for Those Who Want to Give it a Go

Jackson's Lane

269a Archway Road, N6. Tel (0181) 341 4421

Comedy of all sorts is at the forefront of the programmes at this well-known community arts centre. It is possible to see some great acts here, but Jackson's Lane is really best known for the comedy workshops that have been held on its premises. Some of the funniest comics on the circuit today kick-started their careers by taking classes at Jackson's Lane − the burinng question is, do you have what it takes?

Cookery Courses

Can't boil an egg? Is Spaghetti Bolognese a mystery? Then a cookery course may be in order. It's time to tantalise your friends' tastebuds for a change rather than totally disgusting them. It could be a career move or, at worst, a relationship-saver!

Best for Entertaining
Leith's School of Food and Wine

21 St Alban's Grove, W8. Tel (0171) 229 0177

Prue Leith, the school's founder, believed that intelligence and application rather than in-born talent are the keys to being a good cook. The school is now owned by Carol Waldegrave, who upholds this idea as well as the ethos that fresh food is more important than complicated methods. Leith's offer evening cookery lessons for anyone desperate to learn. There are huge waiting lists for courses and pupils are divided into two groups: beginners and advanced. Expect to make dishes such as mustard grilled chicken and millefeuilles with mango and passionfruit sauce. Ten lessons cost £310 for beginners and £320 for advanced.

Best Italian
Tasting Italy

Sara Schwartz, 97 Bravington Road, W9. Tel (0181) 964 5839

Imagine spending time in Italy being taught how to cook by well-established chefs. Sounds like a dream. Tasting Italy offer week-long courses in Piedmont, Tuscany or Sicily, where sun-ripened fruits and vegetables complement the local fresh fish and where you will not just stand and watch the experts, but be encouraged to create such dishes as pasta with truffles or roast figs with honey and orange zest. Accommodation, food and wine are all included in the price, which varies from £750 to £900 depending on your chosen destination.

Best Vegetarian
La Cuisine Imaginaire

Roselyne Masselin's Vegetarian Cookery School, 78 Goldhawk Road, W12 and 18 Belmont Court, Belmont Hill, St Alban's. Tel (01727) 837 643

This is the place to learn about vegetarianism for the 1990s. Nut loaves and curried lentils have no place here and the emphasis is just as much on style and presentation as on the food itself. There are a variety of fun one-day courses on offer such as 'Alternative Christmas Cuisine' and 'French for Fun'. One-day courses cost around £50.

Best for Your Career
Tante-Marie School of Cookery

Woodham House, Carlton Road, Woking, Surrey. Tel (01483) 726 957

Ideal for people who already know how to cook but want to impress their friends and family further. The school offers a one-term certificate as well as a two-term intensive diploma in cordon bleu cooking. There are five kitchens, named after various regions in France, each of which can accommodate up to twelve students. The courses cover British as well as French cuisine and will guarantee people lining up for a chance to eat at one of your dinner parties.

49

Cor-blimey Caffs

There is nothing like a greasy fried breakfast with mugfulls of sweet tea to shake you awake after that heavy night out. Ambience is a big part of the appeal of the local café and the characters and dramas that you can eavesdrop on make Kathy's 'caff' in Eastenders seem positively tame.

Best for Comfort Food
The Star Café

22 Great Chapel Street, W1. Tel (0171) 437 8778

Soho is filled to the gills with busy film and media types. With high-stress jobs and deadlines to meet sometimes only a bit of comfort-eating will help you put yourself back on the road to sanity. The food is basic but steaming hot and plentiful, and you can get breakfast and lunches here. For those on a sugar low they have all the favourite 'school' puddings on offer and once you have swallowed a few mouthfuls of crumble and custard you are bound to smile and start to de-stress.

Best for a Double Life
Bedlington Café

24 Fauconberg Road, W4. Tel (0181) 994 1965

Come to the Bedlington Café for breakfast and then return here at night for dinner. Don't worry – you won't be eating a good old English breakfast twice in 24 hours. By night the Bedlington Café reinvents itself as a Thai restaurant. It has been a hugely successful venture and has collected a regular following of customers who no longer feel the need to eat at home at all. Book for a chance to sample their Thai food and then bring your date back for breakfast the next morning.

Best for the English-Breakfast Connoisseur

Benji's

157 Earl's Court Road, SW5. Tel (0171) 373 0245

For those with a huge appetite and a desire for all the trimmings, the Builder's Platter is a must. Chow down on eggs, bacon, fried bread and baked beans and listen to the hum of conversation going on around you. Take your time and enjoy your surroundings as you sip the free tea and coffee which goes with your meal.

Best for Late-night Cravings

The Market Café

5 Fournier Street, E1. Tel (0171) 247 9470

Who needs daylight? Drag yourself from your bed and follow your nose as the smell of frying bacon draws you towards the doors of The Market Café. The food here is not to be missed and has a home-cooked appeal. The café caters mainly for the poor souls who work night shifts and is open from 2am until lunchtime. Eat here and you are guaranteed a ride home from one of the many taxicab drivers munching down a full English breakfast.

Best for People-watching

Peter's Restaurant

59 Pimlico Road, SW1. Tel (0171) 730 5991

This place is packed with a cross-section of society. Cabbies and builders sit chair-to-chair with lords, but all are united in their appreciation of the food. Starting the day off with breakfast here is a religion for some. Heads are down while people chew and gossip.

Dance Teachers

If you're desperate to impress your friends or just frustrated that your parents never pushed you into dance classes when you were younger, there is no time like the present to start again. Choices are wide and varied in London and classes cater for everyone, whether you want to mambo, rock'n'roll or dance on your pointes.

Best Classical

Anna du Boisson

16 Balderton Street, W1.Tel (0171) 629 6183

This class is tough but also the best-attended open classical dance lesson in London. You definitely have to be advanced enough as well as talented to keep up with not only Anna but the professional-dancers that participate. If you feel the need to brush up on your skills before one of her classes, her colleague Teresa Kelsey is on hand to help beginners and elementary students. The opportunity to take one of Anna's classes is usually enough to spur most people on to work that little bit harder.

Best Contemporary

Bill Louther

16 Balderton Street, W1.Tel (0171) 629 6183

If you've ever dreamed of starring in 'Fame' this is probably the closest any of us will get to the real thing. Bill Louther, graduate of the New York School of the Performing Arts, is considered to be a living icon, having taught such great names as Rudolf Nureyev and Sir Peter Maxwell-Davies. He has set up camp at Danceworks and has his own company, The Dance and Theatre Corporation. However, don't be daunted, he believes that dance is for everyone and that classes should be looked upon as a step to a performance. Professional dancers come to him to keep up to scratch.

Best Flamenco

Zandra Escudero

Tel (0171) 727 8801

Zandra Escudero can make the most unlikely participant simply ooze the spirit of flamenco. Effort is the number one priority in this class; flamenco may look daunting but this controlled dance form can make everyone look elegant when it is mastered. Zandra is a miracle in herself, having been crippled at the age of 14 but going on to become a professional flamenco dancer at 16.

Best Rock'n'Roll

Kav Kavanagh

Tel (0181) 859 3055

This former British Champion teaches with an incredible amount of passion and enthusiasm and is the undisputed king of authentic 1950s rock'n'roll. After only one lesson you will be able to perform quite a few impressive moves and after a few months you will look positively professional. To master moves such as the Pendulum and the Death Slide a one-to-one private lesson is a must.

Dinner-party Caterers

Whether you are having one person to supper or one thousand, deciding what to cook is a minefield. What should you make? How should you make it? Are your guests kosher, vegetarian, or prone to various allergies? Banish the stress and let a dinner-party caterer do the worrying for you.

Best for American-style Munchies

Lox, Stock And Bagel

Flat 4, 51 Drayton Gardens, SW10, Fax (0171) 244 6061 for menu. Tel (0171) 835 2143 to order

Sometimes a dinner date can lead to breakfast or even brunch. So what is the answer if your fridge is bare? David and Janet Evans have come up with the unique idea of delivering American breakfasts direct to your door. For the unbelievably reasonable price of £15 a dozen fresh, chewy bagels and some of the most unbelievable toppings will arrive on the doorstep along with fruit juice and a morning paper. Spread your bagel with chocolate chips or a dill and mackerel mousse, or settle for the traditional option and go for cream cheese and slices of smoked salmon. Telephone as late as 4am and they will still take your order for same-day delivery.

Best for Attentive Service

Gorgeous Gourmets

Gresham Way, Wimbledon, SW19. Tel (0181) 944 7771

This business has been going for 15 years and the friendly and helpful service they offer is supreme. They will cater for parties of any size but they are especially adept at catering for large numbers. There is no set notification time for informing them of your big event but it depends on the time of the year as to whether they can accommodate you. They will travel anywhere in London and the Home Counties and have been known to go as far afield as Jersey. All kinds of diets are catered for and the cost of the food for a three-course meal for 20 guests starts at around £23 per head.

Best for Masterchef Catering

The Contemporary Catering Company

19 Harbord Street, SW6. Tel (0171) 385 3671

A finalist on Masterchef in 1993, Ross Burden now runs his own successful catering company and has been tantalising the tastebuds of many with his wide and varied menus. He will make dinner for two or even cater for that drinks party with the ever-expanding guest list. A visit to your home will be made before the event to discuss the menu. Dinner costs around £30 per person depending on the number of guests.

Best for Wild and Wacky Presentation

By Word of Mouth

22 Glenville Mews, Kimber Road, SW18. Tel (0181) 871 9566

This large catering company has been going for 20 years now. They are extremely popular, will take on jobs from all over the country and abroad for any number of guests, and always liaise closely with the client. Their presentation is imaginative and upbeat and their outstanding decorations will make your cocktail party a talking point for weeks to come. They also hire out staff and dinner services. Food for a dinner party for 14 works out at about £28 per head.

Discount Outlets

There is a discount for everyone and everyone wants a discount - if only they knew where to go. Everything from candlesticks to Christian Lacroix can be obtained more cheaply when you are in the know.

Best for Continental Designer Labels

Discount Dressing

39 Paddington Street, W1. Tel (0171) 486 7230 and branches at:
16 Sussex Ring, Woodside Park, N12. Tel (0181) 343 8343
521 Cranbrook Road, Gants Hill, Ilford, Essex. Tel (0181) 518 3446
164 Queen's Road, Buckhurst Hill, Essex. Tel (0181) 559 1025

This company sells clothes mainly by European designers with prices up to 90 per cent less than those in retail outlets. An agreement with their suppliers prevents them from advertising brand names but they are definitely not short of top labels.

Best for Dressmaking Material

Joel & Son Fabrics

77-81 Church Street, NW8. Tel (0171) 724 6895

Mr. Joel has been in business for 43 years and has a shop in the heart of Church Street Market. Inside, well-known names, including Cerruti, Christian Lacroix, YSL, Gianfranco Ferre and Valentino, adorn the bolts of cloth. Some of the fabrics have been made up by the couturiers into outfits while others are samples from couture collections. Prices range from £4.90–£400 per metre.

Best for Kitchen Equipment
Buyers & Sellers

120-122 Ladbroke Grove, W10. Tel (0171) 229 1947

Selling bargain electrical kitchen equipment, this business has been going strong for 40 years. They deliver free of charge throughout the country and are able to find any current model available at realistic prices. They have a lot of goods at half price and you can make credit card purchases by telephone.

Best for Silver and Silver Plate
David Richards & Sons

12 New Cavendish Street, W1. Tel (0171) 935 3206

The cost of silver here is the same as that of silver plate elsewhere. They work as a wholesaling operation and are able to sell at much-reduced prices. On the ground floor there are solid-silver decorated picture frames, cutlery, clocks, wine coolers, candlesticks, jewellery boxes and pepper grinders. In the basement there are baskets, bread knives, candelabra and ink pots.

Best for Soft Furnishing Fabric
Corcoran & May

157 and 161 Lower Richmond Road, SW15. Tel (0181) 788 9556

Corcoran & May have two shops in Putney and one in Kent. The Putney branches are packed with curtain and upholstery fabric from leading designers such as GP & Baker, Monkwell, Colefax & Fowler, Christian Fishbacher, Charles Hammond and Parkertex. The fact that the shop's stock is made up of seconds, overstocks and clearance lines is reflected in the prices which are generally in the range of 30 per cent to 50 per cent off the original price.

Dog Groomers

Pooch-pampering is big business these days, but it is very important to send your beloved animal to well-trained, professional staff. Grooming can be a traumatic experience for a pet and if you get it wrong the poor thing may be put off for life. When choosing the right establishment, you should look for a City and Guilds certificate which ensures your pet is in capable hands.

Best for Accessories
George of Chelsea

6, Cale Street, SW3. Tel (0171) 581 5114

A very fashionable establishment smack-bang in the middle of swinging Chelsea, this shop will groom your dog or cat to the strains of melody radio. George feels that the soothing music helps the animals to relax and enjoy the experience. There is also a lot of pet-related artwork for sale and commissions for portraits can be undertaken by local artists. Customised dog baskets and hand-made collars and leads are a popular sideline. George is known by locals as the Nicky Clarke of the dog world. His prices vary depending on the condition of the animal, but on average you should expect to part with £25, which includes nail-clipping, ear-cleaning and teeth-cleaning.

Best for Anything
Paws for Perfection

6, Clay Corner, East Worth Road, Chertsey, Surrey. Tel (01932) 566 366

The owners of this establishment are award-winning showers of poodles, so they know all about perfection. Since they trim and groom rabbits and Guinea Pigs in addition to dogs and cats, the summer months are very busy. Prices range from £15 upwards for dogs; prices for other pets are negotiable. Good range of accessories on offer.

Best for Christmas

Mucky Pups

62 Station Road, North Harrow. Tel (0181) 863 7220

Dog owners in North Harrow, it seems, are determined that their pooches should look smart for Christmas. Twenty-five dogs a day can pass through these premises in the run-up to Christmas and New Year. A large range of doggy accessories are sold here and prices range from £17-45 including VAT. The husband-and-wife team have been in the business for over 20 years and their experience shows.

Best-known

Peter's Posh Pets

50 Blythe Road, W14. Tel (0171) 602 1357

Peter Young, the owner of this establishment, which has been running in Olympia for 15 years, is held in high regard by fellow pet-groomers. Princess Michael of Kent sends her cats here. The highest standards are maintained and Peter is not above giving owners a bit of a 'wigging' if he feels that the animal's coat shows signs of neglect. Sensible accessories, as well as food, are sold on the premises. Prices start at £10-12 and can rise as high as £40-50 if the animal is in a truly dreadful condition.

Best for a Laid-back Atmosphere

Handsome Hounds

123 Valetta Road, W3. Tel (0181) 743 5619

Stuck in a backwater between Shepherd's Bush and Acton this dog-groomers is a little domain of peace and tranquility. A happy atmosphere prevails and the staff are keen, attentive and jolly. They have a useful range of basic accessories. Prices range from £10 for a small toy breed in good condition to £50 for a breed such as a very matted and mangy Old English Sheepdog.

Dog Walks

Keeping a dog is a good way to make new friends in what is sometimes an unfriendly city. When you are dogless, people pass you in the street without the slightest flicker of acknowledgement; stick a pooch on the end of a lead, however, and Londoners will automatically brighten. Taking your faithful hound for a walk can lead to firm friendships, not to mention a chance to explore the captital's finest sights whilst getting yourself into shape.

Best Pub Walk
Riverside, Hammersmith to Chiswick

If a quiet pint and a walk by the river appeal, one of London's best walks is the stretch of the Thames from Hammersmith to Chiswick where you can see elegant Georgian houses and beautiful London gardens that back on to the river. Both The Blue Anchor and The Old Ship pubs will allow dogs providing they are on a lead and well behaved. A little further west near Kew Bridge The Bull's Head, The City Barge and The Bell and Crown are all picturesque pubs that will let dogs in at their discretion.

Best for Walking off the Lead
Richmond Park, Surrey

A beautiful tract of almost wild countryside and only six miles from the city centre, Richmond Park is known for its deer, which seem undaunted by the presence of visitors. Dogs can run for miles in this park but it's probably not the place for tiny dogs unless they are very hardy.

Best with Children
Battersea Park, SW11

There are plenty of sights here to keep the children occupied while taking Rambo for his walk. There's a semi-permanent fairground, a zoo, a herb garden, a boating lake, tennis courts and playing fields. Should dog or child wander off, there is a charming police station by the bandstand. If you just want a quiet stroll, may I suggest 'The Peace Mile', a beautiful walk along the river past the Tibetan Pagoda.

Best for Royal-spotting
Kensington Gardens

The adjacent Kensington Palace, designed by Sir Christopher Wren, is home to a whole gaggle of royals and flunkies. Indeed, the Princess of Wales has been known to rollerblade with the public just outside the royal enclave. The activities of would-be rollerbladers have recently been curtailed by the gravel laid on many of the paths after a fatal accident last year. However, Rover won't mind as there is less likelihood of him becoming another fatality. Dogs are allowed off the lead here.

Best Sights for Dog Owners
Silver Jubilee Walkway

Not strictly a treat for Fido, this one, as you will come in and out of lead restrictions. But if your dog doesn't mind being on a leash and you are feeling very fit this walk covers 12 miles of glorious sights taking in Bloomsbury, Euston Station, the Barbican, St Paul's Cathedral and the Bank of England. The last leg of the journey, known as the Queen's Walk, takes you from Lambeth to Southwark Bridge and on to Tower Bridge. A good map of the walk can be obtained from the London Tourist Information Office.

Dress Agencies

You've read about it in magazines, and you've seen the beautiful people wearing it, but where can you get that little black dress that you love at a price you can afford?

Best for 1960s Gear
Salou

6 Cheval Place, SW7. Tel (0171) 581 2380

This shop is filled to the gills with designer cast-offs from women who get new wardrobes for every season. It is popular with tourists and everything in the shop is of flawless quality. The vintage 1960s gear is particularly good. Designer wear includes Chanel, Versace, Armani and Valentino, as well as Donna Karan jewellery and Chanel belts. The shop is somewhat cluttered but the staff are helpful.

Best for Coats
Dress You Up

182 Battersea Park Road, SW11. Tel (0171) 720 2234

Run for the last four and a half years by Yvonne Fitzgerald this wel laid-out shop has a good selection of designer wear including Valentino and Yves Saint Laurent. Coats are an excellent buy, along with sheepskin jackets, suede and leatherwear. There is also a wide range of shoes, belts, bags and scarves.

Best for Leatherwear and Chanel
Pandora

16-22 Cheval Place, SW7. Tel (0171) 589 5289

Clothes by different designers are arranged in separate sections in this spacious shop. Its wide range means that there is something here for everyone. They have an excellent leatherwear rail as well as many ballgowns and cocktail dresses, and this is the place to go for those of you who are dedicated to Chanel. Examples of the goodies on offer include a black Versace tasselled dress for £70 that would retail elsewhere for £800.

Best for Special-occasion Dresses
The Fashion Clinic

180 Wandsworth Bridge Road, SW6. Tel (0171) 736 4425

Shirley Shelley, the owner of this establishment, specialises in evening wear and outfits for those special occasions. She buys new, to guarantee quality, from designers such as Jenny Packham and Terence Nolder. Typical items on offer are long velvet column dresses, elegant long skirts and embroidered jackets. Some of the jackets are designed by Shirley herself.

Best for Swimwear and Suits
Dynasty & Dynasty Man

12 and 12a Turnham Green Terrace, W4. Tel (0181) 995 3846
63 Kensington Church Street, W8. Tel (0171) 376 0291

Selling nearly-new designer clothes, Dynasty have two branches in W4, one stocking womenswear and one menswear, plus a recently opened womenswear outlet in Kensington. Top of the range swimwear for women includes Trulo and La Perla. A Louis Feraud suit costs £110, a Guccci handbag £49 and a Chanel dress, originally £1,000, retails at £150. The men's shop is excellent for Armani suits which are all under £100. Dunhill ties are available from £6. Customers here are mainly in their 20s and 30s.

Dressmakers

Most people have walked into a party confident that their new dress from the hippest shop in town will make them stand out from the crowd, only to realise that at least ten other people in the room are wearing exactly the same frock. To ensure originality next time round, head for a dressmaker.

Best for Aristocracy
Gerald Kane

15 Hillersdon Avenue, Edgware, Middx. Tel (0181) 958 7078

Gerald Kane takes great pride in his work and cuts the cloth himself rather than using other people's patterns. He has dressed some of the the grandest aristocrats in the world as well as many actors. He has a small base of regular clients who appreciate his passion for different types of material. Expect to pay from £750 for an evening dress.

Best for Bright Colours
Robinson Valentine

Mills Yard, Hugon Road, SW6. Tel (0171) 384 1476

Viscountess Linley is a woman to watch, according to the fashion world, and she has given this place her seal of approval. Antonia Robinson and Anna Valentine run the show and delight their customers with their bright and fun colours. They have also brought their business into line with today's technology by relying on computerised pattern cutting. A dress will set you back about £500.

Best for Eye-catching Designs
Angela Stone

257 New Kings Road, SW6. Tel (0171) 371 5199

Angela Stone always has at least one dress on display in the window of her shop which inevitably entices the passing customer. Her dresses are beautifully made and are especially in demand for Ascot. Evening dresses cost between £300– £1,000. If you want one of her colourful short dresses, expect to pay around £175.

Best for Natural Fabrics

Favourbrook

19 Piccadilly Arcade, London SW1 (0171) 491 2337

Although Favourbrook sell off-the-peg clothes, specialising in men's waistcoats, Nehru jackets and other eastern-inspired garb, they will also make any of their clothes up to suit the customer. The choice is wide and fairly exotic with the most delectable variety of beautiful natural fabrics. Fittings are professionally undertaken. Expect to pay around £400 for a velvet Nehru jacket lined in pure silk. Excellent for men's wedding waistcoats and women's evening jackets.

Driving Schools

Passing your driving test can be an awful trauma for some and a piece of cake for others. Hopefully the right teacher should ensure success whatever your standard, but the burning question is, where do you go to find them?

Best for Disabled Drivers
Banstead Mobility Centre

Damson Way, Queen Mary's Avenue, Carshalton, Surrey. Tel (0181) 770 1151

These courses are designed as refreshers and are tailor-made for drivers and novices alike. The lessons cost £14 each and accommodation is provided at £10 per night. Many of the clients here are those who have become disabled later in life and assessments are made to find the best type of driving controls suitable for each individual. If Carshalton is too far for you to travel, the Banstead Mobility Centre will consult the Disability Tuition Register to give you details of instructors throughout the country.

Best Intensive Course
EP Training

The Old Library, Lower Shott, Leatherhead Road, Great Bookham, Surrey. Tel (01372) 450 800

If you don't want to drag the ordeal of learning to drive out over weeks and months then this intensive course is ideal for you. They have an off-the-road training area which they will send you out on before you have to tackle the main road. Each day you are expected to undertake eight hours of driving, with your test being taken on the last day. The course costs £386.63 and pupils commute to the school every day from Waterloo or stay the week in local hotels. The pass rate is 85 per cent for younger drivers and a little lower for older drivers.

Best for Motorbikes

Metropolis

62 Albert Embankment, SE1. Tel (0171) 793 9313

Where motorbikes are concerned, this place has the lot. The basic CBT test can be taken for free if you buy your bike from them, otherwise tuition costs £42 per day with £30 extra for bike hire. They boast a 90 per cent pass rate. Instructors include a policeman, a stripper and a member of the cast of Starlight Express.

Best School

Monk Driving Tuition

175b North End Road, W14. Tel (0171) 385 0707

Colin Monk has been running this school for more than 30 years, achieving a pass rate for his pupils of around 80 per cent. Many famous people have passed through the hallowed portals of his school but Colin refuses to reveal names, except for one – the young Lady Diana Spencer, a former pupil of whom he is very proud. There are eight instructors, including two women, and lessons cost £15.50 per hour between 9am and 5pm and £17.80 at other times.

Best for Young Drivers

Early Drive

The Activity Centre, Brands Hatch, Longfield, Kent. Tel (01474) 872 367

No one is too young to learn how to drive here as long as their feet can touch the pedals. The Early Drive Lesson lasts two and a half hours and costs £45. Lessons after that, named Early Drive Gold, cost £35 per hour. Parents can attend, but choose a day where there is a race going on, giving you something to watch. It is guaranteed to be less nerve-wracking then seeing your own child on the track.

Dry-cleaners

Dry-cleaning should be a fairly straightforward experience. You throw food down your clothes and take them to the nearest dry cleaners. However, each outlet can vary hugely in quality and price, so do a little research first.

Best for Miracles

Valentino Dry Cleaners

Unit 5, 125 Shaftesbury Avenue, WC2. Tel (0171) 240 5879

Owner Maria Datta is called the 'miracle worker' and those in the know, including Paul Smith and the Vogue magazine team, would no doubt agree with this statement. She takes in leather, suede, evening gowns, silks and delicate fabrics all at a same-day service and offers free collection and delivery. Prices: suede skirt £23, leather coat £30, leather skirt £27, suede trousers £29, leather trousers £35, men's two-piece suit £9.50, men's shirts £2, leather coat £45.

Best for Silks and Beads

Buckingham Dry Cleaners

83 Duke Street, W1, Tel (0171) 499 1253

Buckingham's are recommended by, amongst others, the BBC's Clothes Show, MTV and the Vidal Sassoon Road Show. They also specialise in wedding gowns and waxed jackets. The usual time-span for dry-cleaning is two to three days, but jobs can be completed in matter of hours in special cases. Dresses from £9.50, gents trousers £5.50, blouses £5.99 and suits £10.50.

Best for Speed
DeLuxe Cleaners

30 Brewer Street, W1. Tel (0171) 437 1187

Deluxe Cleaners offer a two-day, two-hour or one-day service. Local fashion houses such as Aquascutum, Simpson's, Austin Reed and Dickins & Jones recommend them. Prices: day dress £7.85, evening dress £12.50, silk blouse £4.70, suede skirt £22, leather trousers £35, men's two-piece suit £9.50, jacket £5.50, trousers £4.

Best for Stuffed Shirts
Mayfair Laundry

Stirling Road, W3. Tel (0181) 992 3041

TV and film companies with period costumes to clean send them here. Mayfair Laundry is also patronised by many Jermyn Street shirtmakers. The laundry was established in 1860 and the equipment is old but essential for finishing to perfection such items as stiff collars and dress shirts. Prices (not including VAT): day dress £8.35, evening dress £19.80, blouses £6.20, men's two-piece suits £10.85, jacket £7.30, trousers £5.42. Minimum charge £5.75.

Best for Valeting
Jeeves Of Belgravia

8-10 Pont Street, SW1. Tel (0171) 235 1101

Jeeves take great care with your dry-cleaning, even going as far as wrapping and folding your garments in tissue paper. They clean wedding dresses, curtains, rugs and upholstery and will even dry-clean soft toys. Prices: day dress £16.25, silk dress £21.45, blouse £7.45, men's two-piece suit £15.75, trousers £7.35, jacket £8.40, jacket re-waxed/cleaned £51.45, suede jacket £50.75.

Fancy Dress

Some people are lucky enough to have the creative flair to transform an old dishcloth into a stunning Marie Antoinette ballgown. For those of you without the time or inspiration, do not panic, there are plenty of shops to numb the pain of having to make the outfit oneself.

Best for All-round
Harlequin
254 Lee High Road, SE13. Tel (0181) 852 0193

Harlequin hire out children's as well as adults' costumes, from prices starting at £14 and rising to £30. They also have a noticeboard where a variety of entertainers advertise their services. Open Monday, Tuesday and Thursday 9.30am–5.30pm, Wednesday 9.30am–1pm, Friday and Saturday 9.30am–6pm.

Best for Choice
The Costume Studio
6 Penton Grove, off White Lion Street, N1. Tel (0171) 388 4481/837 6576

This studio boasts the widest choice in London, so if you don't find your ideal oufit here you won't find it anywhere. They have more than 5,000 different costumes and for a minimum charge of £25 you can rent one for a week. Open Monday–Friday 9.30am–6pm, Saturday 10am–5pm.

Best for Tarzan Outfits
Escapade
150 Camden High Street, NW1. Tel (0171) 485 7384

There are 1,500 costumes to choose from in this Camden shop. Hire charges range from £10 for a Tarzan costume to £25 for the highly popular 'ostrich jockey'. Women can pour themselves into beautiful period dresses, which cost £25 for four days' hire, but be warned: if the dress gets stained you will lose your deposit. Open Monday–Friday 10am–7pm, Saturday 10am–6pm, Sunday 12am–5pm.

Best for Luvvies

Angels & Bermans

119 Shaftesbury Avenue, WC2. Tel (0171) 836 5678

This is one of the oldest fancy-dress hire companies in London and the stock comes entirely from film and theatre productions. There are thousands of costumes here, spanning the ages. The minimum charge for a week's rental is £60, there is also a deposit of £100 to pay. Open Monday–Friday 9am–5.30pm.

Best for Value

Regan's Carnival Warehouse

12 Sundridge Parade, Plaistow Lane, Bromley North, Kent.
Tel (0181) 460 1223

This party warehouse is home to more than 2,000 different types of costume. With so much choice and reasonable prices they are almost unbeatable. Three days' costume rental costs from £12–£18 and there is also a wide range of masks of your favourite politicians and members of the royal family. So why not cheer up your bank manager at your next meeting by turning up wearing a mask of the Duchess of York? The shock may be so great that your overdraft may not seem so bad after all. They also sell a huge range of party accessories catering for a wide variety of tastes. Open Monday–Friday 10am–6pm, Saturday 9am–5pm. Closed on Wednesdays and Sundays.

Final Send-off

Since you are involved in every aspect of your life, why stop at death? Your resting place will probably be the last decision that you make so why not consult a funeral director who will respect your last wishes for lying in state? And don't worry, the British are getting better at talking about death. No longer is the subject brushed under the carpet. Indeed, some funeral directors today can be positively jovial.

Best for DIY
Heaven On Earth Mail Order

47 Picton Street, Montpellier, Bristol. Tel (0117) 942 1836

A coffin can seem such an extravagance; who needs a glorified container when they're six feet under? Paula Rainey-Croft has come up with the marvellous idea of doubling-up a coffin's uses. Her mother's coffin (happily not needed just yet since she is very much alive) is currently being used as a bookcase. Paula has also created linen chests as well as spice racks out of what will eventually be someone's last home. The price of a coffin starts at £150 and it is also possible to buy animal coffins from her Bristol shop.

Best for Frozen Assets
F.A. Albin & Sons

52 Culling Road, Rotherhithe, SE16. Tel (0171) 237 2600

It's hard to accept that death is the end. What if sometime in the future they discover immortality? At F.A. Albin & Sons they will freeze your corpse and replace your bodily fluids with a concoction containing rosewater and glycerine for the sizeable sum of £17,500. This means immigration after death since your body will be stored at 197°C below zero in Michigan, USA. If you can't face the prospect of waking up in a strange land many centuries from now, then they also handle 'normal' funeral arrangements.

Best for Last-stop Shopping
Funeral Centre
43-47 Rushey Green, Catford, SE6. Tel (0181) 695 0999

Choosing all the accessories to dress up a funeral can now be as easy as going to the supermarket. At the Funeral Centre there is a wide range of coffins on show and some are decorated in football colours or with Chinese dragons. Wreaths can be made up in the shape of almost anything you fancy and bereavement books are on sale to calm the emotional shopper. If that it is not enough to soothe your cares away, the air is filled with music and the aroma of scented candles.

Best for Pets
Silvermere Haven Pet Cemetery
Byfleet Road, Cobham, Surrey. Tel (0181) 546 7591

A Cornetto box at the back of the garden is not always the most dignified resting place for your favourite pet. At this nine-acre pet cemetery, home to more than 2,000 permanent residents, there is a beautiful, peaceful atmosphere. A cat is usually considerably cheaper to bury than a dog, depending on size, and a marble headstone will cost approximately £250 for the former and £600 for the latter. Cremations are £52 for a cat and £88 for a dog and this price also includes collection of the remains.

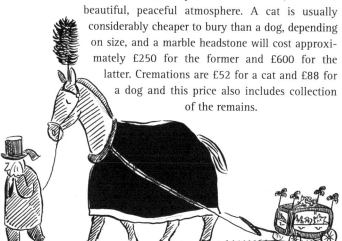

Florists

Late for dinner, or did you forget completely? Then a bunch of flowers could save you from an eternity of silence and sleeping on the sofa huddled up with little more than the dog blanket for company. And what about that obligatory bunch of roses on Valentine's Day? Or your mother's birthday? The simple answer is, don't forget! But if you do, here are a few suggestions for flowers that will make grovelling so much easier.

Best Funky Florist

T. W. Dunn

229 Fulham Palace Rd, London SW6. Tel (0171) 386 5001

Tommy Dunn's clients include Michael Jackson, Mariah Carey and the offspring of Sony, Phonogram and EMI. He loves bunches of rununculas and cut hyacinths – starting at £15 per bunch – but is more than happy to create floral extravaganzas, as he did for the launch of Michael Jackson's History album party. The occasion was marked by a boat gliding down the Thames adorned with one of Dunn's more exotic arrangements, complete with the pop star himself protruding out of the top.

Best for Indulgence

Kenneth Turner

19 South Audley Street, W1. Tel (0171) 355 3880

Kenneth Turner's glorious floral creations may be more expensive than most but they are certainly worth the extra money for their wonderful individual style. We're talking serious statements here; an offering from this master craftsman is guaranteed to melt even the frostiest of hearts or pacify the dourest of Duchesses. A beautiful hand-tied bouquet of fresh flowers costs from £40 and a rose topiary tree from £95. Delivery charges are from £5.50 for central London.

Best for No Frills

Veevers Carter

The Chelsea Gardener, 125 Sydney Street, SW3. Tel (0171) 352 7658

A simple posy of violets costs £10.50 and will no doubt be welcomed by the Eliza Doolittle lookalike you fell for last night. For those who want to be understated and romantic into the bargain, or for the downright mean, a single red rose is only £5.50. Prices are exclusive of the £5 delivery charge.

Best for Quick Deliveries

Garlic & Sapphire

Tel (0171) 585 2124

To beat the Valentine's-Day rush, place your orders in advance to ensure that the love of your life gets their mandatory token. Prices range from £20 to £50 and bouquets have dramatic names such as 'The Unrequited'. Boxed flowers cost from £30 and a miniature 'garden' costs upwards of £40. For those who are guaranteed to forget or are simply feeling very romantic or affluent, there are standing-order weekly and monthly deliveries. Minimum orders are £25 (including delivery) for bunches and £50 for special events.

Best for Something a Little Different

Jane Packer

56 James Street, W1. Tel (0171) 586 2766

For flowers with that little bit extra, Jane Packer, who created Fergie's wedding bouquets, is renowned for her individual and distinctive style. Add a velvet tassel or a scented candle to a single red rose and you might get lucky. A specially designed terracotta pot for Valentine's day is sure to extract a loving 'aahhh..' from the focus of your attentions and will set you back about £35. Delivery is extra.

Furniture Restorers

The cat has clawed your sofa to ribbons and someone broke the arm when falling on it in a drunken haze. Don't put it out for the bin men just yet – send it to a furniture restorer who will nurse it back to health. Prices are given on inspection.

Best for Friendly Service
Adam & Sheridan

7 Ashbourne Parade, Finchley Road, NW11. Tel (0181) 455 6970

This business has been run by Gordon and Valerie Healy for nearly 20 years. They offer a wide range of services, including re-covering, re-upholstering and repairing antique and modern furniture. They have a collection and delivery service but suggest you bring in the smaller jobs as it will work out cheaper in the long run.

Best for General Repairs
S. & H. Jewell

26 Parker Street, WC2. Tel (0171) 405 8520

It feels like the staff here actually want to help you. They will tackle even small jobs and are particularly good at repairing upholstery, mending cabinets and polishing.

Best for Gilding
Rupert Bevan

40 Fulham High Street, SW6. Tel (0171) 731 1919

In this amenable workshop the staff create and design gilded and painted furniture. This labour-intensive craft is fascinating to watch as ordinary furniture is transformed into masterpieces. The brightness of your furniture can be toned up or down according to your wishes.

Best for Leather
K Restorations

1-3 Ferdinand Place, NW1. Tel (0171) 482 4021

This well-established firm charge realistic prices for patching up, reviving and re-covering all your ageing leather-covered furniture. For those who want to try their hand at it themselves they sell a DIY re-leathering kit, and if you make a mess of this, you can always bring your furniture back for the professional treatment.

Best for Wooden Chairs
The Chair Man

1 Baronsmead Road, Barnes, SW13. Tel (0181) 748 6816

Woodworker Richard Homes, who has been in the business for 20 years, can be trusted to work wonders on all those chairs you gave up on years ago. He sees no job as too trivial or too small. While he doesn't undertake larger jobs such as repairing upholstery, caning or rushing he is quite prepared to glue joints or mend breaks on everything from kitchen chairs to genuine Chippendales.

Golf Clubs

Those of us who have never played golf before get great pleasure in taking the St Michael out of all those ghastly patterned jerseys that golfers seem to wear. This is all very well until, after a long-overdue medical, the doctor insists we take more exercise, and we may find ourselves having to eat our words. After all, what better way to unwind after a hard week in the office than a gentle round of golf, and why travel when there are a whole host of decent greens within easy reach of central London?

Best for Central London
Highgate Golf Club
Denewood Road, N6. Tel (0181) 340 5467

Only 25 minutes from Harrods (depending on the traffic) this challenging golf course is London's most central 18-holer. Tight and undulating, the course is well known for its number of long par-4s. Visitors are welcome from 9am to 3pm (or after 3pm with a booking). A handicap certificate is required. Green fees are £27 per round or £35 a day.

Best for the City
Royal Blackheath Golf Club
Court Road, Eltham, SE9. Tel (0181) 850 1795

A mere eight miles from London Bridge, with a 300-year-old clubhouse, this attractive parkland course peaks with an 18th hole that needs a pitch to the green over a clipped hedge! It sounds more like the Grand National, but it's well worth a shot if golf's your bag. Competent weekday visitors are welcome, but ring first with your handicap certificate. Green fees are £40 a day and £30 a round.

Best for Points North

Moor Park Golf Club

Rickmansworth, Hertfordshire. Tel (01923) 773146

This club, which boasts a 17th-century club house, hosted the Bob Hope Classic in the early 80s on its two 18-hole courses. They're a bit sniffy about amateurs but welcome competent golfers. Green fees are £55 per day, High Course is £35 a round, West Course is £25 a round.

Best for Points South

Coombe Hill Golf Course

Golf Club Drive, Off Coombe Lane West, Kingston, Surrey.
Tel (0181) 942 2284

Described by Henry Cotton as, "one of the most delightful settings for a golf club I have ever experienced anywhere in the world," these grounds are enhanced with spectacular displays of rhododendrons at every hole. Designed in 1911, this is one of the most exceptional courses built early this century. Competent players are encouraged and welcomed for weekday visits but a handicap certificate is required. Green fees are £45 a round or a day; £25 after 3pm.

Best for Points West

Royal Mid-Surrey Golf Club

Old Deer Park, Richmond-on-Thames, Surrey. Tel (0181) 940 1894

Right next to Kew Gardens and the River Thames, this is London's most popular golf course, thanks to its beautiful parkland location and spectacular 18-hole course. Membership is restricted, but week-day visitors are welcome. You should contact the pro first with your handicap certificate. Green fees are £45 a day or £20 after 4.30pm if you can make a dash from the office.

Grocery Deliveries

You can buy your clothes, furniture and jewellery from the television shopping channel or over the phone, so why not have your groceries delivered to your door as well? Indulge in the ultimate in laziness and pick up your phone (if you can manage that much).

Best for Flexibility

Universal Aunts Ltd.

19 The Chase, SW4. Tel (0171) 738 8937

You can send Universal Aunts all over London to do your shopping for you. Ring them up with an order or ask a member of staff to make a home visit. If you weigh them down with shopping, however, you will have to pay their taxi fare for them. The most usual requests they get are for basic foods such as fruits, vegetables and potatoes but they say they are up for anything! Ring for a leaflet about their services.

Best for Gourmets

The Pie Man

23 Pensbury Street, SW8. Tel (0171) 627 5232

If you are looking for something a bit more exotic than a slab of chocolate and a tin of baked beans, pop into The Pie Man. They will fill your own containers up with cheeses, meats and freshly prepared supper dishes. They even stock peanut butter and jelly in a jar? They will deliver in central London for a £5 charge. Minimum order £25.

Best for Grand Groceries

Fortnum & Mason

181 Piccadilly, W1. Tel (0171) 734 8040

Fortnum & Mason deliver on a daily basis to central London and on specified days to the Home Counties. For those expats who crave English delights, Christmas hampers can be sent anywhere in the world. They will try to accommodate unusual requests, such as sending a fish pie to France. Delivery costs £4 but is free if you spend more than £50.

Best for Italian Food and Funghi

Carluccio's

28A Neal Street, WC2. Tel (0171) 240 5710

If you dream of pesto and polenta or you pour olive oil on to your food as freely as water flows from a tap then this is the place to order your food from. Even an Italian wedding cake is available here. Carluccio's will deliver to addresses in central London and Dulwich. There is also a mail-order catalogue. Delivery charges £4–£8.

Gyms

So you want to look like Pamela Anderson on acid or Sylvester Stallone on steroids? Help is at hand in the manicured sweat boxes of the capital.

Best for Families in West London
The Hogarth Health Club

1a Airedale Avenue, London W4. Tel (0181) 995 4600

A green oasis in the suburban backwaters of leafy Chiswick, The Hogarth offers two outdoor tennis courts, a squash court, pool and gym. It incorporates a health clinic that provides alternative therapies and an in-house doctor and dietician. Crèche facilities are available with qualified nannies, which makes it perfect for families.

Best for Ladies who Lunch
The Peak

Hyatt Carlton Tower, 2 Cadogan Place, SW1. Tel (0171) 235 1234

Fill your carrier bags at Harvey Nicks and Harrods, stuff your face at Marco Pierre White's and then stagger up to the ninth floor of the Hyatt Carlton Tower hotel to sweat out your hangover and keep your facelift in shape. Full membership is £1,250 a year, plus £250 joining fee, which enables you to sample The Peak's sunbeds, saunas and treadmills. This club is great for the Harrods helmet brigade and Euro White-trash.

Best for Lounge Lizards
Champneys

Le Meridian Piccadilly, 21 Piccadilly, W1. Tel (0171) 437 8114

Bang in the basement of the luxury Le Meridian hotel, in the heart of the West End, this temple of neo-classical calm centres around the stunning swimming pool that attracts the bodies beautiful and the wallets bountiful. A full range of beauty treatments, squash courts, a gym and a personal trainer at no extra cost leaves the others standing in terms of pampering. Full membership is £1,512 per year, plus £250 joining fee, but hotel guests can use the facilities for free, so why not book in for a wild night out and spend the following morning getting back into shape?

Best for Rubber-necking

The Harbour Club

Watermeadow Lane, London SW6. Tel (0171) 371 7700

If you want to perfect your pecs with Princess Di or curl your abs with Will Carling in security-guarded splendour this is *the* place to do it. But, inevitably, it doesn't come cheap. For the pleasure of dipping in the navy, womblike swimming pool, playing on one of the 14 tennis courts or taking advantage of the excellent wine list, you will have to part with a cool £2,500 a year, plus £175 a month or £10,500 for life membership. For the socially aspirant, it's no doubt a price worth paying – where else can you chuck back the Chablis to cool down your sweating brow as Hugh Grant, Oliver Hoare, Kate Menzies and Amanda Wakeley drift by?

Best for Whizz-kids in the Sauna

Cannons

Cousin Lane, London EC4. Tel (0171) 283 0101

After a £3 million state-of-the-art refurbishment, Cannons is the place to start moving those muscles with stressed-out stockbrokers intent on keeping their adrenalin at bay in the six squash courts, two pools, three gyms and 80 exercise classes a week. Make no mistake, Cannons is serious - luxury lapdogs need not apply to join. Prices are £175 plus £560 a year which, if shaping up your body and wallet is on the agenda, seems very good value.

Hairdressers

You've just broken up from your boyfriend or have finally managed to jack in the husband. You feel the need for a complete change of image, or just a bit of pampering, so a trip to the hairdressers is a necessity. Or you may be a normally adjusted human being who feels that a trim, wash and blow-dry are in order.

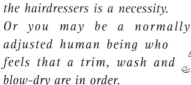

Best Cup of Cha

Andrew Jose

1 Charlotte Street, W1, Tel (0171) 323 4679

All tastes are catered for here from a cup of typhoo to a watery tisane. For those with a sweet tooth there is chocolate on offer. Colourings are a speciality and Nicola Clarke, the queen bee, experiments with a painstaking range of shades to suit her clients' colouring, building confidence before taking the plunge. Other services include a seasonal make-over with in-house make up artist Charlie Duffy. Cuts from £25-£60.

Best Fittings

Carvers

50 Maddox Street, W1. Tel (0171) 629 9951

The careful attention given to the decoration of this shop is a good indication of the attention they will give to your hair! If you like what you see in the mirror you can not only pay for the cut, but the mirror as well. Eamon Murray, owner and passionate antique collector, also sells glass, china, lamps, silver and paintings which adorn his salon. Their Victorian mirrors cost around £80, while other artefacts start at £25. Cuts from £25-£35.

Best for Gossip
DAR Hair and Beauty

8 Broxholme House, New Kings Road, SW3. Tel (0171) 736 2893/2268

Cutting and styling are the specialities of the house. However, Dar, Steven, Patrick, Alan and Bruce are the five good-time boys who run the joint and are also experts in making a trip to the hairdressers feel like a good party. Gossip and amusing stories fly round this relaxed, and friendly setting. You may go in there looking a fright but you are guaranteed to come out with a hairstyle that suits a smile on your face and a wealth of stories that would keep Nigel Dempster's column running for a year. Cut and blow-dry £20–£35.

Best-looking
Stephen Way

109 New Bond Street, W1, Tel (0171) 493 5304

This hairdressers has been luring well-heeled clients for over 25 years. The 58 year-old owner is claimed by many loyal clients to be the dishiest and best-looking hairdresser in London. A pioneer of modern-style hairdressing, Way has earned himself the title 'King of the Crimpers'. Way introduced the hugely popular Paul Mitchell products to this country, which many top models swear by. For those with drastic needs that need discreet attention or aspirant Garbos who just want to be alone, there are private rooms. Favourite 'luvvie' clients include Melanie Griffiths, John Hurt, Tara Fitzgerald, Tom Ogilvie and, perhaps saintliest of all, Ian Ogilvie. Cuts from £28-£60.

Happy Hours

The thought of Happy Hour may seem a bit passé these days, conjuring up images of secretaries getting hammered on Malibu and Pinapple and throwing up on the bus on the way home. Nonetheless, real value for money can still be found in many bars around London at the bewitching hour.

Best for Cocktails
Smollensky's On The Strand,

105 The Strand, WC2. Tel (0171) 497 2101

If an up-front, brash cocktail is what you are after, then make a trip to Smollensky's for Happy Hour from 5.30pm–7pm during the week. The cocktails are half-price and served with plenty of gusto. A Happy Hour piña colada costs £2.25 and if you're nursing a hangover, a Bloody Mary may be just the answer at £2.

Best for a Beano
The Boardwalk

18 Greek Street, London W1. Tel (0171) 287 2051

Drink one, get one free, seems to be the order of the day here. Happy Hour lasts from noon–2pm, Monday; noon–2pm and 5pm–7pm, Tuesday and Wednesday; 5pm–8pm, Thursday and Friday; 6pm–7pm, Saturday. Although prices are higher than those of a pub, this joint also offers a live disco, which plays to a packed dance floor in the basement until 3am, on Thursday, Friday and Saturday.

Best for Bubbly
Michel's

122 Wardour Street, W1. Tel (0171) 287 0204

Every night is Happy Night here at Michel's in Wardour Street. So if you want to beat the blues by imbibing some bubbles, cheer yourself up between 5pm–8pm, from Monday to Saturday by downing a bottle of half-price Angas Brut. If only the real thing will do, take heart, a bottle of house Champagne will set you back a mere £10.98 – a price you would find hard to beat even at your local off-licence.

Best for Gringos
Salsa
96 Charing Cross Road, WC2, Tel (0171) 379 3277

Speedy Gonzales had better get his skates on for Mexican Monday Happy Hour at this popular venue, where ten tequilas are £1 per shot, with free admission all night, 25 per cent off food, and where you can dance off the effects with a trained Salsa expert. After 9pm, admission is £3 on Tuesday and Thursday, £5 on Friday and Saturday. Open until 2am, every day of the week with live music every night.

Best Piano Bar
Baboon
Jason Court, 76 Wigmore Street W1. Tel (0171) 224 2992

Although the name suggests otherwise, this bar is rather stylish and sophisticated. Happy Hour is from 5.30pm–7pm, Monday to Friday, and you can get slaughtered on house wine for the very reasonable price of £5.95 a bottle, beer at around half price or a delicious piña colada at a mere £2.50. If, after all that, you are feeling a bit peckish there is a restaurant attached with food at a reasonable price.

Hat Shops

Whether you are going to Ladies' Day at Ascot or have to don a respectable number for great-aunt Maude's funeral, a hat can really put the finishing touch to an outfit. Hats can be worn by just about everyone, from Audrey Hepburn lookalikes to Nora Batty clones; you just need a little bit of confidence to carry it off.

Best for Elegance
Gilly Forge

14 Addison Avenue, W11. Tel (0171) 603 3833

By appointment only

Gilly Forge started off designing hats for friends before setting up her own business. Her hats are second to none for elegance, and Gilly is, incidentally, very good-looking herself. Hats take about a week to make.

Best for Old Hat
David Shilling

10 Marylebone High Street, W1
Tel (0171) 487 3179 or (0171) 262 2363

By appointment only

David Shilling's designs used to be rather wacky back in the 1970s and 1980s but he has toned down his style somewhat for the 1990s. His hats are always made from beautiful fabrics but are astronomically expensive.

Best for Tea Parties
The British Hatter

36 Kensington Church Street, W8. Tel (0171) 361 0000
Open Tuesday-Saturday 10am-6pm

A small, but very good shop selling hats designed by owner Nick Wheatley as well as men's hats by Christy's and Tessi. Prices start at around £12 and rise to £125.

Best for Trend-setters
Philip Treacy

69 Elizabeth Street, SW1. Tel (0171) 259 9605
By appointment only

What can you say about Philip Treacy? He's very famous, has an outrageous style, and his career is most certainly on the up. He is also the recipient of numerous fashion awards and makes hats for Chanel, Valentino and Karl Lagerfeld. He also has his own shows. Busy man.

Best for Variety
The Hat Shop

58 Neal Street, WC2. (0171) 836 6718

This well-known establishment has been trading for over 15 years. There is a huge variety of both men's and women's hats on offer and prices range from as little as £2.50 to £250. You can either pick up a funky street fashion beret here or a staid mother-of-the-bride affair – this shop caters for both ends of the spectrum. They are also good at restructuring old hats or retrimming new ones. As the shop is so small, the staff sometimes have to restrict the number of customers entering at one time – so avoid the Saturday rush in the summer months, as men and women of all ages descend upon the shop to find their wedding hats.

Health Food Shops

If you can't face the thought of exercise but still want a healthier lifestyle, why not check out a few health food shops, for years the preserve of ageing hippies in search of vitamin supplements. Don't worry, you don't have to be a vegetarian. Just be open-minded as you scan the shelves.

Best All-rounder

Wild Oats

210 Westbourne Grove, W11. Tel (0171) 229 1063.

Wild Oats is considered the king of health-food stores and owners Jan and Stephen work hard to maintain their standards. Shelves and aisles are easy to negotiate and a whole range of organic fruit and veg is beautifully displayed along with an amazing range of breads. Those on macrobiotic and coeliac diets will find all they need here, as well as plenty of good advice. For the boozers amongst you, they even stock organic alcohol which, we are assured, won't give you a hangover. A likely story.

Best for Bread and Nuts

Bumblebee

30, 32 & 33 Brecknock Road, N7. Tel (0171) 607 1936

Business has been booming since Bumblebee opened in 1980 and they have since opened two more shops. One of the outlets is now predominantly a nut shop, with various grains and pulses making up the rest of the stock. There is always a queue of people next door waiting for their fresh bread and vegetarian foods while across the road is the third shop, which sells organic fruit and vegetables. All three shops make for a one-stop shopping venture and the staff are helpful to boot.

Best for Muesli

Neal's Yard Wholefood Warehouse

21-23 Shorts Gardens, WC2. Tel (0171) 836 5151/379 8553

For muesli connoisseurs this is the place to go, sample and buy. The shop also stocks a wide range of dried fruits, large amounts of nuts and that old standby, peanut butter. For those who are a bit more daring, there is a selection of vegetable root 'crisps'. Pickle lovers should try the mango chutney and there are a wonderful selection of soft drinks available.

Best for No Additives

The Real Food Store

14 Clifton Road, W9. Tel (0171) 266 1162

For those allergic to artificial additives and flavourings this is the place to stop off. Careful attention is given to the quality of the food prepared and stocked in the shop by owner and former chef Kevin Gould. In addition to the healthy grains and fruits on display there is a wide selection of 'gourmet' foods. And if you are feeling peckish while shopping, they have a takeaway section where you can buy food to eat at home (although you may not get much further than your own car before tucking in).

Best for Wholefoods

Wholefood

24 Paddington Street, W1. Tel (0171) 935 3924

This shop, the pioneer behind wholefoods in the 1960s, is somewhere not to be missed. You will get all your basic health food, including pulses and grains. On a more exotic level you can buy sea vegetables, bancha twig tea and nut butters. They have taken a great deal of care over labelling all their products and it is well worth taking the time to peruse the shelves.

Homeopathic Remedies

Do you ever get the feeling that if you take any more prescription medicine you will turn into a chemical waste dump? Homeopathic remedies cure almost any symptom that you can imagine and are free from the traumas of side effects.

Best Energy Booster
E'mergen'C

The massive injection of vitamin C in a sachet of E'mergen'C is a great way to avoid colds and 'flu if, of course, you can afford to take one every day. For us poorer folk it is ideal to take as an energy booster when the engines are burning low. If you're still sceptical don't forget that it has been recommended by the models that walk the catwalks in Paris. We must, after all, follow fashion! This particular remedy is loaded not with vitamin C but with all the B vitamins you can imagine and is apparently laced with 25 different electrolytes. And we can all do with more of those... £2.90 for six sachets.

Best Sinus Soother
Clinarome

Using Vicks or Karvol to clear your nose is like declaring to the world that you feel off colour. To some the smell is a comforting one but others want something that can disguise the fact that they are not feeling their best. Spray Clinarome on to your handkerchief or pillow at night and you will not offend your partner or stain your clothes. Its pleasant and soothing smell comes from a mixture of neroli oil, lavender, mint and thyme. £4 for a 50ml atomiser.

Best Stress-buster
Bach Rescue Remedy

This floral- and brandy-based infusion really works – trust me. It will soothe your nerves while you prepare to take off in a plane, or calm you down before that big interview. Among the 39 different varieties of stress busters on the market ,this is the real McCoy. £2.40 for 10ml.

Best Tonic
Floradix

For those who seem to be constantly tired from the stresses and strains of everyday life an early night should normally remedy the problem. However, if you are still left yawning, you may be suffering from an iron deficiency. Floridex is one of the most complete iron supplements available and is an aqueous extract of 20 herbs and vegetable and fruit concentrates, with added B vitamins and minerals. It's ideal for combatting drooping eyelids. £5.99 for 250ml.

Hotel Bars

The hotel bar is the place to hire and fire, meet and greet, or embark on an illicit affair. The anonymity provides protection against unwanted intrusions as most people are slightly embarrassed about being seen in one and because they're so public, rubber-necking is out of the question.

Best for Boozing with a View
Windows

28th floor, Hilton Hotel, Park Lane, W1. Tel (0171) 493 8000

This is where 007 might take his leading lady for a pre-espionage unwinder. It's where Mr Smoothy Chops takes Ms Sexy Knickers. The panorama over Hyde Park is stunning. Watch the more energetic members of the human and equine race trot down Rotten Row as you knock back the ubiquitous Martini – shaken not stirred. For £6 nightbirds are welcome to prop up the bar from 11pm until 2am.

Best for Players
The American Bar

The Savoy Hotel, The Strand, WC2. Tel (0171) 836 4343

The American Bar at the Savoy Hotel is glamorous, serious and sexy, perfect for expense account players who've come to wheel and deal with the big boys. We're talking Sir James Goldsmith and Sir Andrew Lloyd-Webber here (Lord Lucan would if he could). Not that it's stuffy – the service is superb. Discretion is the bar staff's watchword and they've probably seen it all. Considered by many to mix the best Martini in town, The American Bar charges £7.50 for the pleasure and shuts at 11pm, which discourages serious benders. Its glamorous interior is decked out in the style of a 20s cruise liner.

Best for Singles

The Bar at 190 Queensgate

The Gore Hotel, SW7. Tel (0171) 581 5666

Good music and a sexually active atmosphere attracts a well-heeled, hot-to-trot crowd every weekday night. This is a place to kick off your work shoes and get into the serious business of meeting and greeting the opposite sex. If you don't get lucky you can always slink into one of the seriously deep sofas, drink your troubles away and end up staring into the bottom of a well-mixed Margarita at £6, until 1am weekdays and 2am Friday and Saturday.

Best for Treats

The Palm Court

The Ritz Hotel, Piccadilly, W1. Tel (0171) 493 8181

Stumble into the Palm Court after lunch at Le Caprice, or have a G and T with Great Aunt Agatha at £5.25. This place is a melting pot for treats of all sorts behind the gilded portals of The Ritz, evocative of elegant times gone by and a stylish way of life that is hard to find in the busy streets of modern London.

Best for Serious Style

The Downstairs Bar

Blakes Hotel, 33 Roland Gardens, SW7. Tel (0171) 370 6701

It's dark down there, but Anouska Hempel's somewhat dated style temple still draws in glamorous, Gucci-clad go-getters who think nothing of blowing £8 on a Bloody Mary. Visiting imbibers might include luvvie hellraisers such as Mickey Rourke and Rupert Everett – it's bad boys' territory, but who's complaining?

Hotel Bedrooms

There is nothing lovelier in the whole wide world than staying in a really good hotel. It must be at least as comfortable as your own home – skimp on this and you miss the point entirely. The staff should be quiet and efficient and, while not being obsequious, should automatically agree with you if you point out that something is wrong (like a husband).

Best for Beds

The Savoy

The Strand, WC2. Tel: 836 4343

Hotels are all about beds and at The Savoy they take them very seriously. In fact, they make them themselves, to the most exacting standards, and if you like yours enough you can buy it. You might want to try the room on the fifth floor were Monet stayed and painted over 70 versions of the view down the Thames from the window. Rates start at £230.

Best for The Belle Epoque

The Ritz

Piccadilly, W1. Tel: 0171 493 8181

Cesar Ritz built this camper-than-Christmas shrine to extravagant French style in 1906. The bedrooms are decorated with the same

Belle-époque flourishes as the common parts, but you must leave your bed, however briefly, because the dining room is the prettiest in London. Truman Capote said it was when he realised that death is the central aspect of life that he learnt to drink champagne and stay at the Ritz. And you could stay here for quite a while as the bedrooms have gorgeous walk-in wardrobes and the hotel is well located. Rates start at £190.

Best for Conservatories
The Berkeley
Wilton Place, SW1. Tel: 0171 235 6000

As a hotel must be at least as comfortable as a home, it could be that you cannot do without a conservatory of your own. Don't fret, The Berkeley has three rooms with their own private conservatories, including their plushest apartment called The Wellington Suite. The hotel is built on the site which was once the parade ground of the First Regiment of Foot Guards who were to fight and win the Battle of Waterloo under the Duke of Wellington's leadership - hence the theme. There is even a portrait of the Duke in the sitting room. Rates start at £255.

Best for Romance
The Sloane Hotel
29 Draycott Place, SW3. Tel: 0171 581 5757

This tiny hotel, which opened only a year ago, has the most romantic bedroom in all London. Room 202 has a French canopied bed, draped in silk and piled high with antique linen pillows. Even the ugliest frog should turn into Prince Charming in this environment. There are only 12 rooms and suites and they have been individually decorated and furnished so that there is none of that nasty feeling of portion control that lurks around the big chains. And if you like your room you can buy the entire contents. Everything is for sale. Rates start at £125.

Ice-cream

A '99' from a Mr Whippy van is the staple diet of most children, but when you grow up your tastebuds become a little more sophisticated. As the years go by even the chocolate flake poking out of the side can't disguise the mushy mess of chemicals masquerading as ice-cream. So for those with more delicate tastes and a desire to keep the children free of chemicals, here are the best places to find ice-cream worthy of your flake.

Best for Creaminess

Criterion Ices

118 Sydenham Road, SE26. Tel (0181) 778 7945

This no-nonsense, old-fashioned ice-cream parlour may be slightly off the beaten track but, believe me, it's worth it. Prepared by the Valenti family, the ice-cream is a combination of Italian and British influences and is made from such luxurious ingredients as Cornish clotted cream and Jersey double cream. This is one of the few places where you can still buy real vanilla ice-cream. A scoop costs 80p and a sundae £3.

Best for Families

Marine Ices

8 Haverstock Hill, NW3. Tel (0171) 485 3132/485 8898

All those wise to the delights of ice-cream come to Marine Ices. You are just as likely to see a financially strapped student with a spoonful of ice-cream in hand as a bored, rich housewife dripping with diamonds. The Mansi family have been doing a roaring trade since 1930 and they now sell their ice-cream to 1,500 other restaurants. On Sundays the restaurant is packed with frustrated weekend dads trying to keep on the good side of their children. A scoop of their delicious ice-cream will set you back £1.20 and a sundae from £2.30 to £5.50.

Best for Nostalgia

C. Notarianni & Sons

142 Battersea High Street, SW11. Tel (0171) 228 7133

The third generation of this ice-cream-making family have expanded the business into a pizza restaurant where they serve the best calzones in the city. The ice-cream, still dominant on the menu, is served from an antiquated Italian dispenser and is not to be missed. The décor merges past and present and gives you plenty to look at as you savour the heavenly ice-cream. A scoop costs £2.50, a sundae £3.50.

Best Old-fashioned Gelateria

Foubert's

162-168 Chiswick High Road, W4. Tel (0181) 995 6743
Richmond Italian Bar, 39 Kew Road, Richmond, Tel (0181) 332 0348

This place is not to be missed – a little slice of Italy come to Chiswick offering you the most delicious ice-cream. Owner Luciano Lo Dico has been making ice-cream for more than 20 years. His ice-cream, which is prepared fresh on a daily basis, will tantalise your children's tastebuds and have them running away from rather than towards the average ice-cream van. A child's cone costs 85p.

Best for Shoppers

The Fountain Restaurant at Fortnum & Mason

Piccadilly, W1. Tel (0171) 734 8040

For those godparents who are unused to children but somehow got conned into looking after them for the afternoon, this is the perfect watering hole. Here you can indulge the little treasures in the most incredible sundaes and when they have feasted on too much chocolate you can send them home to their parents with a tummy-ache. That should save you from another babysitting job for at least a year. All sundaes cost £4.25.

Interior Restoration

Wear and tear is an inevitable part of domestic life. No matter how careful you are around the home, things do get broken, marked and sometimes even burnt. Nothing is more annoying than breaking a plate from your favourite dinner service or snapping a stem from one of your best wine glasses. So, where do you go to get your treasured possessions repaired and restored? Here are some really useful places - get out your address book now.

Best for Glasses

R Wilkinson & Son

5 Catford Hill, Catford SE6. Workshop Tel (0181) 314 1080.
Delivery/collection address: 1 Grafton Street, W1

Wilkinson's have been a glass repair act for three generations. They now hold the royal warrant and David Wilkinson heads a team of 18 craftsmen. Over half their customers are private individuals bringing in mainly heirlooms and pieces of sentimental value. Services include grinding chips off wine glasses (£5 to £10); or putting a new foot on a wine glass (approx. £25). They also have vast stocks of spares, and are often able to match stoppers and liners (in blue or clear glass), or make new ones. Stained glass can be cleaned and even dishwasher-dulled crystal can be repolished. They also clean, restore, rewire chandeliers and restore antique mirrors and metal work. Repairs take from two to four weeks although an intricate chandelier could take up to four months

Best Parquet People

Campbell Marson

Wimbledon Business Centre, 34 Riverside Road, SW17. Tel (0181) 879 1909. Main Showroom: 573 King's Road, SW6. Tel (0171) 371 5001

This old-established family-run firm, now headed up by Pippa Marson, has been supplying parquet floors for over 70 years. They offer a full restoration service for London's beautiful old floors - parquet (usually oak) is particularly prevalent in Kensington, Knightsbridge and Chelsea. They'll take up broken pieces, match and fix replacements, re-sand the whole floor, and finish with two to three coats of suitable lacquer. They need about seven to ten days notice; work takes up to five days. Cost is around £15 to £20 per square metre, but a new floor could cost £100 per square metre.

Best at Putting Back the Pieces

China Repairers

64 Charles Lane, NW8. Tel (0171) 722 8407

"We much prefer a clean break", says Virginia Baron cheerfully. "We hate cracks, they are difficult to repair satisfactorily". She heads a team of five experts at a workshop that's been trading for over 40 years. Modern glues mend most china these days – ugly riveting is old hat. Basically there are two levels of repair: a "stick and touch up" for items which are going to be used; and a full restoration service for decorative items of value. This could involve modelling missing pieces which is a speciality here. Minimum charge is £10, and repairs take anything from a day to four weeks. A month's course as a "working apprentice" costs £1,000; two months costs £1,700.

Introduction Agencies

Are you bored with singles bars where people eye each other up over their glasses of Dutch courage? Time was when dating agencies were unmentionable in polite society but today more and more people are flocking to them for a chance of getting lucky in love.

Best for Brain Power

Drawing Down the Moon

Adam & Eve Mews, 165 Kensington High Street, W8. Tel (0171) 937 6263

This agency is the ideal place for well educated singles to find love. Don't worry, you don't have to have a PhD or even a master's degree, but you will be interviewed before joining. You'll then be invited to put pen to paper and write an introduction about yourself. This will be shown to other members along with your photograph. Unlike most agencies, at Drawing Down the Moon you actually get to choose whom you want to meet, although the staff might stick their noses in if they feel strongly that you are overlooking your possible soulmate. A year on this agency's books will cost you £625 but this figure does include membership to an exclusive dining room. If you sign up on the spot after your interview they will deduct £100 from the joining fee.

Best for International Success

English Rose Introduction Agency/The English Connection

Romance House, 29 Albion Street, Broadstairs, Kent. Tel (01843) 863322

If you have had no success in this country, what about trying abroad? Americans are lining up to write to the average Brit. English Rose caters for English women looking for American men; while The English Connection is for men keen to meet American ladies. All men on the agency's books must be financially secure, with a job, their own house and a car. After filling out a questionnaire you are matched with five people; after that your photograph is circulated among them and anyone can get in contact. Annual membership is £295 for English Connection and £449 for English Rose. Don't fancy a Yank? Well, it just so happens that they have just started an introduction agency linking the UK with Germany and Switzerland. Call the number above for further information.

Best for Party Meetings
Candleburners
105a Moore Park Road, SW6 Tel (0171) 371 5535

If you can't face meeting a blind date on your own with no chance of escape, Candleburners organise Enchanted Evenings where members can mingle until they find that special person. Owner Cheryl Brown personally interviews every applicant and looks for socially confident, attractive professionals. She has a knack of unearthing those who say that they are single but are actually married. A years' membership costs £650 and this will ensure 12 to 15 introductions. If Enchanted Evenings are more your style then a payment of £200 entitles you to join in any of their 35 events a year.

Best for Wrinklies
Katharine Allen Marriage Bureau
18 Thayer Street, W1. Tel (0171) 935 3115

If you feel that you are too old for a conventional dating agency and you're looking for a more mature partner then this bureau, established in 1960, is where it's at. An initial interview costs £17.50 and if you decide to join after your friendly grilling then you pay a further £500 for the first year. After that it costs £125 a year and £250 if you get married through the agency.

Launderettes

Launderettes used to be dreary places run by Dot-Cotton-lookalikes with fags permanently dangling from the corners of their mouths. The atmosphere was grim, the clientele mostly the poor getting poorer as their DSS money was gulped up by defective machines charging inflated prices, and the only diversion was watching great-aunt Hilda's bloomers become entwined with Uncle Albert's combinations. These days, London's launderettes, with their state-of-the-art machinery and Conran-influenced décor are more likely to double up as community centres, creches and steamy chat-up joints. It cannot be long till we follow our American cousins' initiative and introduce 'washaramas' complete with bars, sunbeds et al.

Best Welcome

Bubbles

196 West End Lane, NW6. Tel (0171) 794 2107

There's a genuinely nice atmosphere in this launderette based in one of London's most cosmopolitan areas. Watching TV or chatting to manageress Sue and the other friendly staff will ward off any possible outbursts of clothes rage as you wait for your load to finish spinning in one of the fully-modernised machines. A same-day shirt-ironing service is on offer: drop off your clothes before 4pm and collect by 8pm. There's also a dry-cleaning drop-off point. Soap is sold over the counter in packets priced at 60p or there's a kiosk selling larger packets of soap as well as one-wash packs, laundry bags, fabric conditioner, liquid and powder bleach. Staff are always on hand should you need them. Machines: four large (25lb); eight small (16lb) front-loaders; nine dryers, one spin-dryer. Prices: self-service £2 for a 16lb load; £2.50 for 25lb loads; service washes cost an extra 60p or 80p respectively per load, plus soap. Ironing costs £1 per shirt. Open 8am-8.25pm daily.

Best Service Wash

Bobo's Bubbles

34 Connaught Street, W2. Tel: (0171) 262 4659

Lolita, the popular Spanish attendant, has worked here for 15 years and attracts loyal customers from far afield. Staff are in attendance from 7.30am through to 2.30pm daily. Machines: Eleven (16lb); five dryers. Prices: self-service £2; service wash negotiable but usually 60p per load. Open 7am-10pm daily.

Best for Early Birds

Red and White Laundries

64 Lupus Street, SW1. Tel: (0171) 828 3049

No need to worry about having the right coins for this launderette as there is a computerised change machine on the premises. There are no extra frills here, just good honest value-for-money. Staff are in attendance from 8.30am-8pm daily. Machines: three large (25lb), seven small (15lb) dryers Prices: self-service £1.50-£1.70 for 15lb loads; £2.50 for 25lb loads; service wash negotiable with attendant. Open 6.30am-8.30pm daily.

Lidos

Once as chic as a chip butty, Lidos are enjoying a renaissance. A retro fad in favour of municipal architecture plus one of the hottest summers on record has seen thousands flock through their creaking turnstiles. So, when the heat haze begins to shimmer again, grab your lilo and head to a pool near you.

Best for New-age Fun

Brockwell Park Lido

Dulwich Road, SE24. Tel (0171) 274 3088

Unheated

Brockwell was only saved from the bulldozers by the intervention of Patrick Castledine and Casey McGlue who took it over from Lambeth Council three years ago. The whole place was re-decorated with the work of local artists and now boasts a café serving 'Global food' (open 7pm to midnight daily). This summer there will be children's music classes three times a week in addition to the daily 'Kiddies Club' (10am–12pm). The Lido is open from May 4th–Sept 30th. Hours are Monday-Friday 6.45am–10am, then 12pm–8pm. On weekends, hours are 10am–7pm. Fees: adults £2.50, children £1.50, concessions (OAPS, UB40S, students) £2.

Best for Posers

The Oasis

Endell Street, High Holborn. Tel (0171) 831 1804

Heated

The Oasis has indoor and outdoor pools next to each other, so you can rush inside if all that bracing air gets too much. The water is heated to a luxurious 27–30 degrees Celsius, making it possible to swim in winter without risking hypothermia. The laned swimming will please the committed, but wear your best cossie as the pool is overlooked by office blocks and a housing estate. Limited sunbathing room is available. Changing rooms have lockers, hairdryers and showers. Also offers saunas, a gym and exercise classes. Open all year round 7.30am–8pm; adults £2.50, children 75p.

Best for the Real 'Sarf' London
Tooting Bec Lido

Tooting Bec Road, SW16. Tel (0181) 871 3088

Unheated

At over 90m this Lido claims to be the second longest open-air pool in Europe and is certainly one of the grandest – it was built by soldiers after the First World War. Gaily painted rows of huts serve as changing rooms and the café offers hot dogs and hamburgers. Plans are afoot for a paddling pool, but there are no other facilities to speak of. It can get very crowded in summer as adolescent South London struts its stuff in the cramped sunbathing area. Showers are primitive. Open year round to members of the South London Swimming Club, membership is £10 plus £1.50 per swim. Hours are 6am–10am for Club members and 10am–8pm for Joe Public.

Best for Serious or Literary Types
Parliament Hill Lido

Gordon House Road, NW3. Tel (0171) 485 3873

Unheated

This is the Hampstead set's favourite place for a dip (John le Carré is said to be a regular) and a great place for serious swimmers. Set in the middle of Hampstead Heath, it was built in the 30s and retains a faded period charm. There are diving boards, a slide and ample space for sunbathing. Children's inflatables are banned, but there is a small paddling pool. The café is open most of the day and serves ice-cream and hot dogs. Showers are good. The Lido can get busy during the summer – they've been known to have 2,000 swimmers a day. Open first week in May to the second week in September; no charge from 7am–9am, but from 10am–6pm adults pay £1.80, children 90p.

Lingerie

People could sell seats for the spectacle of men buying lingerie for the women in their lives. They duck and dive down the aisles, blush scarlet if they knock anything over and jump a mile in the air if a sales assistant offers to help them.

Best for the Boulder-holder
Rigby & Peller

2 Hans Road, SW1. Tel (0171) 589 9293

Every girl should drop her inhibitions and experience this. You won't recognise your own silhouette after you have been strapped in and pushed up at Rigby & Peller. The no-nonsense sales assistants will tell you what size you really are and not what you aspire to be. Bra sizes start at 32AA and go up to 46FF.

Best for Cotton Undies
Marks and Spencer

458 Oxford Street, W1 and branches across the capital. Tel: (0171) 935 7954

Expats travel back to England to buy their underwear from Marks and Spencer. This is the place to go for reasonably priced, good-quality cotton underwear in a wide choice of pretty designs. While you peruse their camisoles and boxes of colourful knickers your partner can browse around the boxer shorts and briefs.

Best for the Flashy Man
HOM

12 A Foubert's Place, W1. Tel (0171) 434 0627

Men who like to be outrageous pick up their sexy underwear here. Although prices start at £5 for a pair of briefs, they are more often just as extravagant as some of the articles of clothing.

Best for Glamour

Janet Reger

2 Beauchamp Place, SW3. Tel (0171) 584 9360

If you ever want to treat yourself – or someone wants to treat you – then come here. Janet Reger's glamorous and expensive underwear will make you feel like a new woman and more than a little bit special. The most popular lingerie material is silk with a lace trim and items come in a variety of rich and exciting colours. Prices range from £2.95 for a garter to £700 for a silk dressing gown.

Best for Retro

Agent Provocateur

6 Broadwick Street, W1V. Tel (0171) 439 0229

First things first, this is not a Soho sex shop, despite any first impressions you may get when you walk through the door. Co-owners Joseph Corre and Serene Reese have filled their shop to the brim with fabulous underwear with a 1950s retro look. The garments are mainly imported from France and the USA and come in a range of sizes, including larger sizes for well-endowed men. Vivienne Westwood, Joseph's mummy, sells her 'prostitute' shoes here for £230.

Loos

Being caught short in London is no laughing matter. Smelly loos, lack of lavatory paper and dirty hand towels are considered bog-standard in the capital. Well no more! If you pick your pees perfectly it can be an uplifting experience.

Best for a Chance Meeting
Belgo Noord

72 Chalk Farm Road, NW1. Tel (0171) 267 0718

The religious feel of this restaurant follows through into its Ladies rooms. There is only an opaque piece of glass set into the wall that separates you from the mens' next door so it is possible to see a silhouette of the opposite sex. Who knows? It could be comparable to an episode of Blind Date and you may meet the man of your dreams as you both emerge. Then again it could just be a waiter dressed as a monk.

Best for the Feel-good Factor
Claridge's

Brook Street, W1. Tel (0171) 629 8860

This ladies' loo is not without the feminine touch. Floral décor and a wooden finish greet you as you enter. The attendants wait for you to emerge from the cushy cubicles and then present you with a basin filled with warm water and smelly soap. Public loos have notoriously unflattering mirrors, but not here – the lighting is low and a full-length mirror is situated next to the door so you can check that you haven't tucked your skirt into your tights before rejoining the real world. It doesn't matter what age you are, you cannot help feeling a touch Babara Cartland about the whole experience. Largish tip of £1 is expected but not compulsory.

Best for the Movie Interval

Museum of the Moving Image

South Bank, SE1. Tel (0171) 928 3535

At first glance, this may seem like any sterile-looking loo, but it's the background music that gives it its edge. Sitting on the loo, you are seranaded by the shower scene music from the film, Psycho. It must be a crafty ploy on their part to defer tedious queues – and it works.

Best for Winning Prizes

Fan.Museum

12 Crooms Hill, Greenwich, SE10. Tel (0181) 305 1441

In 1993 this place won the Loo of the Year Award. Lest you hapen to forget where your moment of relief is being spent the fan motif is displayed everywhere, even down to the soap. The founder of the fan Museum, Helene Alexander, was advised by Lord Montague, himself an exponent on public entertainment, to "Give people a good museum, a good cup of tea, and a good pee." It seems to have worked.

Best for Your Money

Harrods

Brompton Road, Knightsbridge, SW1. Tel (0171) 730 1234

Forget about spending a penny here, where stingies may feel that paying a pound for a trip to the loo is a bit excessive. It's worth it. Everything just oozes extravagance and the marble and gold interior complements its razzle-dazzle feel. There are free designer scents and luxurious hand towels. You can't leave without feeling just a little bit Joanie (Collins that is).

Mail Order

Sometimes there is no opportunity to peruse the high street stores at leisure. Long hours at work or screaming children make even a lightning dash to the shops an impossibility. Mail order catalogues have stepped into the breach and, happily, we can now buy a wide range of stylish clothes and accessories without leaving home.

Best for Big Women

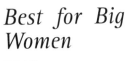

1647

69 Gloucester Avenue, London NW1. Tel: (0171) 722 1647

1647 was founded by Helen Teague and Dawn French to cater for British women of size 16 or over. You will find clothes in a variety of sizes ranging from 16 to 47 (the company name is a clue, here). You can also visit the shop and try the clothes on there. Leggings and tunics are available from £36, lycra bodies from £69 and there is a range of skirts, tunic dresses and trousers from £48.

Best for English Essentials

Bodden's

4 Pembroke Buildings, Cumberland Park, Scrubs Lane, London NW10. Tel (0181) 964 2662

This company, set up by ex-banker Johnnie Bodden, provides well-made English clothes for both men and women. Bodden's also have a warehouse at the above address where you can go and browse, and they provide a tailoring service. Men's and women's cotton drill trousers can be picked up for £45, long-sleeved poplin shirts for £32, shorts for £30. Linen jackets start at £120 and linen trousers at £65.

Best for Men's Shirts
Charles Tyrwhitt Shirts

Freepost, 298-300 Munster Road, London SW6 6YX. Tel (0171)386 9900

This mail-order company sells classic shirts made from Egyptian two-fold cotton poplin; some with pearl buttons. Free brass collar stiffeners are provided. Depending on the level of stock, orders are despatched within 24 hours. Shirts £39, ties from £16.50, braces £26.

Best for the Sporty Look
Swaine Adeney

Freepost, Great Chesterford, Saffron Walden, Essex CB10 1BR.
Tel (0171) 734 4277

This is a chance for city types to kit themselves out for those weekends in the country. There are English tweeds, Scottish cashmere, suede garments and Nubucks. Cartridge bags cost £265 and ladies' shirts are available from £69.

Best for Women's Shirts
Madeleine Hamilton's White Shirt Collection

Mail order department: Tel (0171) 833 3388. Retail outlet: Chichester Rents, Chancery Lane, WC2. Tel (0171) 404 8484

This no-nonsense company was established in 1992 by ex-lawyer Madeleine Hamilton. She can have shirts delivered directly to your office. Prices include £49 for a fine needlecord shirt, £59 for a classic white linen shirt and £120 for a silk/organza blouse.

Makeovers

There are days when even Supermodels look in the mirror and wish it could all be different. Short of plastic surgery, most of us think that there is not a lot we can do about that ugly mug staring back. A makeover can do wonders for the morale and can really change the way you look. In fact you can change the whole way you feel about yourself in a very short amount of time and relatively cheaply.

Best Advice

Glauca Rossi School of Make-up

10 Sutherland Avenue, W9. Tel (0171) 289 7485

This make-up school has been going for six years and has proved very popular with professionals. Ms Rossi's clientele is hugely varied from up-and-coming news presenters to rich society ladies who live in constant fear of being traded in for a new model. Students from the course go on to work on Pop premos, The Big Breakfast and MTV amongst many other popular TV credits. Ms Rossi will also advise clients on a one-to-one basis. Products used are a mixture of her own which are available to buy, as well as other well-known brands. Prices start from £70 for two hours.

Best Lesson

Molton Brown Cosmetics

58 South Molton Street, W1. Tel (0171) 499 6474

You'll find a huge range of cosmetics and colours to choose from in this makeover. The choice is really yours but if you seem to be going off-course professionals will gently guide you towards colours and potions which suit you. Having approved the effect on one half of the face you are then invited to emulate the other side, picking up tips and advice as you do so. Top-quality own brand products used. Prices start from £45 for one hour, £55 for one-and-a-half hours and £30 for a 35-minute makeover.

Best for the Natural look
The Sher System

30 New Bond Street, W1. Tel (0171) 499 4022

The Sher system has earned a deservedly good reputation for its water-based skin saving techniques. Not only will the experts provide solutions on how to cover imperfections, they will also advise clients on the best way to look after a woman's most treasured asset. Women who have never previously worn make-up are encouraged to enhance their best features with a totally natural look so this is not the place for aspiring vamps or heavy metal rock stars, more your mother-earth wholesome look. A questionnaire at the beginning of a session will help determine a regime which suits best. A no-nonsense approach will leave the customer brimming with confidence. Price: £50, redeemable against the company's own products, which have gained world-wide acclaim.

Best for a Total Re-vamp
Stephen Glass at Face Facts

73 Wigmore Street, W1. Tel (0171) 486 8287

Stephen, the chap in charge at this gaff, takes the whole person into consideration when doing one of his makeovers. Be ready to answer questions about your lifestyle regarding wardrobe, current skincare regime, etc. and be prepared for suggestions which you would never have considered in a month of Sundays... Trust him, he knows what suits. A variety of top-quality products are used including Christian Dior, YSL and Prescriptives so he remains unbiased and impartial to what really will give you the best results. You will pay £65 with Stephen or £45 with a lesser mortal.

Manicures

A person's hands, like their shoes, can say an awful lot about them. It is no good getting all dolled up in your best Chanel, Manolo Blahnic if your hands look like monkey appendages. However, no matter how hard they try, some people are left with short flaky nails and rough blotchy skin. If you have the time, money and patience, regular trips to the manicurist can work wonders. For instant glamour and a confidence boost 'permanent' false nails are hard to beat.

Best for Falsies

SuperNail

101 Crawford Street, W1. Tel (0171) 723 1163

These fake nails are so real in appearance that it is not necessary to wear nail polish over the top. SuperNail, run by Carolyn Sears, uses a fine fibreglass mesh, resin, and spray bond to create a clear and flexible surface while your real nail grows behind. A complete set costs £70 but will need maintenance and 'fill-ins' to keep up the look. Great for a special occasion.

Best for French Manicures

Knightsbridge Nail and Beauty Centre

7 Park Close, Knightsbridge, SW1. Tel (0171) 225 3695

Gina Roche's talent is for the natural look inspired by the ever popular French manicure. There are many different shades of varnish on offer and for people who want to be even more indulgent there is a perfumed top-coat that comes in a variety of smells. A French manicure costs £15.

Best for Hand Treats

L'Avenue Decleor

17 Lowndes Street, SW1. Tel (0171) 235 3354

After a trip here, your hands will feel as good as new! For £22 your hands will be exfoliated, toned and massaged with various oils and creams, followed by a soaking in a warm aromaplasm poultice and generous applications of hand cream as you leave. A half-hour experience which really rejuvenates your hands.

Best for Jessica Nails

Elegant Nails and Beauty

Whiteley's Shopping Centre, Queensway, W2. Tel (0171) 792 2233

The American Jessica Vartoughian is the inspiration behind the nail treatment here. The shop, overflowing with treats for your hands, is run by Karen Oliver. The result is a tough and glossy look and although the process takes time the end-product is well worth the wait. A manicure costs £20.

Best for a Quickie

The Green Room

23 Long Acre, WC2. Tel (0171) 379 9600

This environmentally-friendly shop is big on recycling. Staff are happy to tell you what has been used before and you walk away with your own emery board and orange stick. Filled to the brim with Body Shop products it is easy to get carried away here by the huge range of exotic-sounding products on offer. A no-nonsense low-key approach, performed by well trained staff, makes this treatment especially suitable for people who are rushed and harassed. The cost is £13 without varnish and £18 with.

Markets

Bargain-hunting can be addictive and, for Londoners with an eye for a good buy, certain markets are well worth dragging yourself out of bed for on precious weekend mornings. Each market has its own unique style and ambience, which can transport you to a whole host of other worlds. So put on a warm coat over your fluffy bunny pyjamas and get out there for a bit of market culture.

Best for Antiques

Bermondsey Market, Bermondsey Street, SE1.

The old adage, 'the early bird catches the worm' definitely applies here. Customers rummage by torch light as some stalls pack up by 9am. Bermondsey market has been in existence since 1855 and although exciting finds are not seen as often as they used to be, they still exist. The stallholders are keen to dispel the myth that the market is a clearing house for 'hot' items. Customers have been known to uncover incredible bargains, especially when it comes to fur coats (a second-hand mink recently went for a fiver). Silverware sells at a modest price. Open Friday 3am to 1pm.

Best for Flowers and Plants

Columbia Road, E2.

It is impossible to walk away from this flower market empty-handed. The mixture of tempting, vibrant colours and the friendly cajoling of stall-holders, such as Mr Hamett, is irresistible. (Situated on the corner of Ravenscroft Road and Columbia Road, Mr Hamett is well worth a visit.) The flower market has been here for 60 years and is reputed to have sold every kind of plant known to mankind at knock-down prices. Be prepared to buy in bulk and turn your garden into a tropical rainforest. Open 7am–1pm.

Best for Jellied Eels

East Street, SE17

At this market, where everything seems to be on sale, the world is your oyster. The choice is wide and varied and ranges from food and clothes, to those little things that you just can't do without. Above all, do not leave without sampling the jellied eels. Doused in vinegar and served with fresh crusty bread for the rock-bottom bargain price of £1, these fresh eels will convert even the most dubious. Open from Tuesday to Sunday 8am to 5pm.

Best for Organics

Spitalfields Organic Market, Commercial Street, E1.

For those wanting to get back to nature and away from modern pollutants, look no further. The market sells food of only the finest pedigree, nurtured and grown to organic perfection. The prevailing customer is a caring, sharing type; a whole day can be very pleasantly whiled away sitting by the fountain and smiling at all the other happy people with their recycled bags, shopping until they drop. Open Sunday 10am to 5pm.

Best for Two Wheels

Brick Lane, E1.

It's won't be the cars that run you over here but the bikes which, throughout the morning, are given test drives before the cash is handed over. This is the best place in London for those who are looking for a two-wheel bargain. My advice, though, is not to come here if you don't think you can keep up with the cyclist jargon. Open Sundays, 6am to 1pm.

Museums for Children

It's raining, it's pouring, your old man is snoring – and the children's holidays seem to be going on and on! Don't despair, London has an amazing wealth of museums on offer for children that are light-years away from the boring old specimens of yesteryear.

GRRRRR!

Best for Budding Film-makers

Museum of the Moving Image

South Bank, SE1. Tel (0171) 401 2636

Staff dressed in period costume guide you round and keep a smile on your face. You can become a dalek (and even talk like one), watch and make your own film and experience what it feels like to be interviewed by Barry Norman. And, if you fancy yourself as a budding Scarlett O'Hara, there is the chance to audition for a Hollywood film. Great fun. Children £4 and adults £5.95

Best for Button Pushing

The Science Museum Flight

Exhibition Road, SW7. Tel (0171) 938 8008

Launch and design your own space ship, get busy in a hands-on activity room and fiddle with sand that feels like liquid. A flight lab deck enables kids to sit at terrifyingly realistic aeroplane controls. Open 10am–5.50pm. Children £2.60, adults £5.

Best for Creepy Crawlies
The National History Museum
Cromwell Road, SW7. Tel (0171) 938 9123

Attractions are the Blue Whale, countless creepy crawlies, life-size dinosaurs and an Interactive Ecology Department. However it's the dinosaurs that still attract the most attention – children seem to be eternally fascinated by these creatures. Open 10am–5.50pm, Sundays 11am–6pm. Under-17s £2.00.

Best for London Travel Freaks
London Transport Museum
39 Wellington Street, WC2. Tel (0171) 379 6344

The 200-year history of London transport is recounted with interactive videos, real tubes and buses, a Billy Brown London Town Tour, actors reconstructing London travel throughout the years as well as smells and sounds associated with travelling through London. Open every day from 10am–6pm, except Friday when the museum opens at 11am. Adults £4.25, children £2.50.

Best for Sweet Dreams
Bethnal Green Museum of Childhood
Cambridge Heath Road, E2. Tel (0181) 980 2415/3204/4315

A must for nostalgia freaks with quite the best collection of children's costumes, toys, doll-houses, games and puppets in the country. There are also year-round exhibitions that reflect every aspect of childhood. Open Monday–Saturday 10am–5.50pm and Sunday 2.30pm–5.15pm, closed Friday. Admission free.

Museum Shops

Until fairly recently, museum shops used to be rather dreary places selling badly reproduced postcards and dishcloths. Then somebody woke up to the fact that big bucks could be made out of these places – and the museum shop at the Metropolitan Museum in New York was born. London is now hot on the heels of its colonial cousins with some of the finest museum shops in the world.

Best for Cards
The Victoria and Albert Museum

Cromwell Road, SW7. Tel (0171) 938 8500

The Victoria and Albert Museum Shop is home to a really fantastic collection of cards covering nearly every subject under the sun and considered by some to be the best collection in the world. Old favourites such as Tintin, Winnie the Pooh, etc., still continue to sell well. There is also a large variety of handmade cards from as little as £2 each. Open Monday 12am–5.30 pm, Tuesday to Saturday 10am–5.30pm.

Best for Children
The Natural History Museum

Cromwell Road, SW7. Tel (0171) 938 9123

You will find a really remarkable treasure trove of goodies at the Natural History Museum, and you can be sure that teacher would approve as they are all educational and fun. Semi-precious stones and rocks can be purchased from 50p and numerous types of dinosaurs can be bought from 50p to £11. Educational but fashionable T-shirts can be bought for £9.99. Open 10am–5.30pm Monday to Saturday, and Sunday 11am–5.30pm.

Best for Chinaware
The Royal Academy

Burlington House, Piccadily, W1. Tel (0171) 439 7438

A large and beautiful selection of chinaware is on sale at this illustrious institution with limited editions by Royal Academy members such as Elizabeth Blackadder and Michael Kenny, costing from £34.95 to £49.95. Open from 10am–6pm every day of the week.

Best Traditional
The Museum Store

37 The Market, Covent Garden, WC2. Tel (0171) 240 5760.
Also at: 50 Beauchamp Place, SW3. Tel (0171) 581 9255)
and 40 Perrins Court, NW3. Tel (0171) 431 7156

A jolly good all-rounder, this one, with items for sale from leading museums all over the world including the National Archaeological Museum of Athens, the Bulawayo Museum of Zimbabwe and the Bibliothèque Nationale in Paris. A good selection of kitchenware is also available from museums around Britain. Open Monday to Saturday 10.30am–6.30pm and Sunday 11am–5pm.

Best for Jewellery
The British Museum

46 Bloomsbury Street, WC1. Tel (0171) 636 1555

A simply spectacular selection of jewellery, based on copies from originals as varied as Anglo-Saxon brooches made of pewter (£9.95) to Roman filigree gold-plated rings (£34.95), can be found at this museum. There are also lmany reasonably-priced copies of weird symbolic emblems, ensuring fertility or warding off the evil eye. Open Monday to Saturday 10am–4.45pm and Sunday 2.30pm–6pm.

Musical
Instrument Shops

One day you wake up and think move over Mozart, roll over Beethoven, or eat your heart out Mick Jagger. Before you let your imagination go into overdrive, here are a few practicalities to help you on your quest for musical stardom.

Best for Banjos
Barry Dew

20 Chapel Market, N1 9EZ. Tel (0171) 837 0646

For those with an offbeat desire to learn this instrument and earn a role in the re-make of Deliverance, this is the place to go. Not only can you buy a banjo here but you can also get them restored and repaired. Monday to Friday 10am–5pm, Saturday 10am–1.30pm.

Best for Equipment Hire
Peter Webber Hire

110 Disraeli Road, SW15. Tel (0181) 870 1336

Everything can be hired here, from instruments, to disco set-ups and full festival backlines. It is also the home of Ritz Rehearsal Studios, where the likes of Blur have rehearsed. For the budding rock star the shop houses all musical instruments needed to set up a band, and the staff are on hand to give you advice. 9.30am–6pm (by appointment).

Best for Fastest Repairs

Blanks

271-273 Kilburn High Road, NW6. Tel (0171) 624 7777/ (0171) 624 1260

Blanks has an enormous variety of musical instruments. Prices are competitive and the staff are helpful and friendly. There are more than 500 guitars in stock as well as a huge range of traditional Irish instruments. Repairs are done extremely quickly – if you deposit your intrument in the morning it should be ready to pick up the same day. Monday-Saturday 10am-5.30pm.

Best for Windbags

All Flutes Plus

5 Dorset Street, W1H 3FE. Tel (0171) 935 3339

All the different flutes that you could possibly imagine as well as a great range of woodwind instruments can be found here. If you can't play an instrument they have a great range of classical records. The staff are very willing to help and are available to restore and repair instruments. Rental service is also available.

Best for Hippies

The Folk Shop

Cecil Sharp House, 2 Regent's Park Road, NW1 7AY. Tel (0171) 284 0534

Friends of the Glastonbury Festival, this is your paradise! Here you can find strings, reeds and other essentials for your instrument. In fact, if you are feeling very creative there are ready-to-make kits for harpsichord, crumhorns, citterns, and lutes. The starting price is £200. They also have a full repair and restoration service. Monday to Friday 9.30am–5.30pm, Saturday 10am–6pm.

Night Clubs

Whether you're prince or pauper, skint or scrooge, there are an infinite number of nightspots in London to choose from. One can literally spend thousands in a thrice – or for the more thrifty a beer and a bop can last for hours. One thing all nightclubbers have in common is that they all want a great night out...

Best Newcomer
Monte's
164 Sloane Street, SW1. Tel (0171) 245-0891

This slick, up-market nightclub opened towards the end of last year to much banging of drums and rustling of notes. The interior is on three levels comprising a dining-room, discotheque and bar and is decked out in the style of an old, salubrious liner with a marvellous array of wood panelling and veneer. The club is open to the small hours and the music tends to vary according to the taste of the crowd on the dance floor. It's a membership-only club and costs £500 a year to join plus a £250 registration fee. Dinner in the dining room can cost anything up from £75 per head.

Best for Sneaks
Ministry of Sound
103, Gaunt Street, SE1. Tel (0171)378 6528

This revamped venue cost the owners £250,000 to tart up. Recently, the management encouraged customers to ring the police if they suspected any drug-taking in the wake of the Leah Betts ecstacy tragedy, which did wonders for its straight reputation. It's all gone very techno these days and the music is mostly House which is blared out over the world's first digitally-processed club sound system. Drinks are reasonably priced, with one whole bar devoted to vodka. The crowd is young and trendy. Open 11pm–8am; admission £12 for non-members and £8 for members.

Best for Street Cred
The Cross

Goods Way Depot, Off York Way, N1. Tel (0171) 837 0828

This immensely popular venue has been going for nearly three years and grows weekly in popularity, although it is probably situated in one of the grottiest areas in London, notorious for prostitutes, pimps and pushers. However once inside, it's easy to forget the raddled surroundings you've just left behind. The music is predominantly House and Garage and the crowd is mainly young and from North London. There is no food available on the premises unless you order some for a private function and drinks are reasonably priced. The action doesn't really get off the ground till midnight and on Saturdays it doesn't stop till 6am. Open every night except Monday and Wednesday; £12 entry, £15 on Saturday nights.

Best for Toff-spotting
Annabel's Club

Berkeley Square W1. Tel (0171) 629 1096

This long-established members-only club attracts the rich and famous from all over the world and, inevitably, has a long waiting list. However, if you are lucky enough to get invited, you will discover rather a cosy atmosphere emulating that of a private, somewhat opulent house. All activity takes place underground where there are two bars, a dining-room and disco. Music consists mainly of the latest hits (golden oldies are available on request) although you won't find much Ragga or House here. If you do decide you want to join the waiting list you will have to find someone to propose and second you who belongs to the club and who has been known to you for some time... good luck! Membership is £500 per year plus a £250 registration fee and dinner will cost anything from £75 upwards per head.

Paint Shops

Nothing to do this weekend? Then how about doing all those jobs you said you would, like painting the spare bedroom? Painting may be a chore, but you will be amazed at the colours you can now slap on your walls. You can even mix-and-match subtle shades and hues to suit your own taste. In fact, the very sight of a shade card may soon spur you into action.

Best for Artists

Green & Stone

259 King's Road, SW3. Tel (0171) 352 0837

This established picture-framer also deals in paint — from basic acrylics to a very expensive 35ml tube of vermilion for £102.45. Devotees can mix their own paint from pure pigments. Along with discerning house-painters you will find art students pouring in here for their ready-mixed oils, watercolours, and acrylics.

Best for Bargains

Leslux

148 High Road, N2. Tel (0181) 883 9522/2419

Prices are low here, but Tony Sidnick warns you not to look for even lower prices elsewhere, which will prove a false economy. 'You'll only need more coats,' he warns. Leyland gloss and undercoat is £11.99 for five litres, while Johnson's emulsion costs £6.99 a litre .

Best for Fashion Shades

John Oliver

33 Pembridge Road, W11. Tel (0171) 221 6466 and (0171) 727 3735

If you see yourself as a trend-setter or follower, this is the place for you. Owner John Oliver has been bringing people up to date for 30 years. Popular colours include shades of Imperial Chinese yellow and Betty II Blue. A hand-painted swatch of this year's colours, which includes 40 shades, costs £2.

Best for Historical Colours

Paper and Paints

4 Park Walk, SW10. Tel (0171) 352 8626

These people are colour-matching specialists and owner/proprietor Patrick Baty has a degree in the history of paint colours. They have just invested in some colour-matching computer equipment that gives a much closer match than could ever be achieved by the naked eye. There is a mixture of colours to choose from inspired by different times and objects. Matt and silk emulsion retails from £11.63 a litre and eggshell and gloss £13.27 a litre.

Best for Mediterranean Hues

Brats

281 Kings Road, SW3. Tel (0171) 351 7674

The colours here are very vibrant and £2 samples are available so that you can try out a potential choice at home. If you go for the Mediterranean Palette, which is a blend of 29 authentic chalk-based shades from Turkey, you can create something excitingly exotic. A 3.4kg concentrate costs £27.99.

Parks

It is all too easy to forget that London is not, in fact, a concrete jungle. Its many parks are an oasis of greenness and colour filled with the gentle sounds of the English at play (and the not-so soothing hum of rollerbladers careering along paths and walkways).

Best for Bel Canto
Holland Park main entrance

Kensington High Street, W8. Tel (0171) 602 9483
Box office: (0171) 602 7856.
Belvedere Restaurant: (0171) 602 1238

Opera in the park has now become an annual occurrence in Holland Park, and its reputation is spreading. Take a rug and a picnic hamper and dine in style while you listen to favourites such as Verdi's La Traviata and Leoncavallo's I Pagliacci. If you don't want to eat among the peacocks, then the Belvedere is on hand to wine and dine you while you listen to the Opera Europa and the European Chamber Opera.

Best for Car Cruising
Battersea Park

SW11. Tel (0181) 871 7530

This park has it all, from tennis courts and fountains to an adventure playground and a children's zoo. On the last Saturday evening of the month, car enthusiasts arrive to show off their cars and pick up parts. It costs £4 for car owners and starts at 7pm. For enthusiasts this is heaven, and the 'Chelsea Cruise' is a well-established part of park life.

Best for Dinosaur-hunting

Crystal Palace Park

SE19. Tel (0181) 778 9496

Forget Jurassic Park and the bones in the Natural History Museum, this is where the imagination can run wild with dinosaurs living on their own island in the middle of the park. The dinosaurs are left-overs from the landscaping for Crystal Palace when it was moved from Hyde Park to Sydenham Hill. A strictly no-touching attraction.

Best for Romance

St James's Park

SW1. Tel (0171) 298 2000

Perfect for hand-in-hand strolling at the beginning or end of an evening. As the gentle security lighting brings St James's to life at night, the park becomes a very romantic place for strolling and you can smooch from Marlborough Gate to Queen Anne's Gate. If you stand with your loved one gazing into the lake instead of into each other's eyes, you will see the reflection of Buckingham Palace.

Best for Smelling the Roses

Queen Mary's Garden Inner Circle

Regent's Park, NW1. Tel (0171) 298 2000

The sweet smell of roses is incredible here and you can spend hours, with eyes shut, drinking in the fragrance. There are 14,000 roses of different kinds and species adorning the bushes. You can enjoy some that date back to the 1600s as well as newer ones named after famous film stars such as Rex Harrison.

Party Planners

Who's kidding who? Any time is a good time to have a party and, let's face it, someone somewhere out there is doing it tonight... When you've won the roll-over Lottery and it's time for the canapés to hit the dancefloor, you really should know who to call.

Best for Attention to Detail

Fait Accompli

32b Queensgate Mews, SW7.
Tel (0171) 581 0384

Newsagent heiress Kate Menzies and her friend Camilla Leigh-Pemberton run the excellent Fait Accompli. They deal in fab food, blissful booze and an attention to detail that would make a tax inspector swoon. If your little darlings are hell-bent on a swanky teenage rave and you can't face strutting your slightly older stuff till three in the morning, then worry not, these girls will keep an eye on the inevitable festing without a heavy hand.

Best for the I-Threw-This-Together-At-The-Last-Minute Approach

Catherine Owens

33 Brookville Road, SW6. Tel (0171) 610 1698

Catherine describes herself as "a party consultant for people who can't - or won't - organise their own parties but don't want to go to the expense of having a large company to do it for them." Sounds like anyone you know? Well give her a call. There's nothing that you can throw at her that she won't be able to handle.

Best for the Fantasy-party League
Bentleys

26a Winders Road, London SW11. Tel (0171) 223 7900

Peregrine Armstrong-Jones (half brother of Lord Snowdon) does parties like Patsy from Absolutely Fabulous does champagne. Both Elton John and Princess Anne called upon his services for their 40th birthdays (separate parties, you'll be pleased to learn).

Best for an Illuminating Experience
Fisher Lighting and Productions

Unit 1, Heliport Industrial Estate, Lombard Road, SW11. Tel (0171) 228 6979

If you're dreaming of a starry, starry night, these guys are for you. They managed to transform that most sterile of venues, the Grosvenor House Hotel, into an Arabian Palace and gave Diana Ross a wedding party in Switzerland that knocked the socks off her fortunate guests; not to mention George Michael's 30th birthday bash that was rumoured to have been the cause of one enormous collective hangover for days after.

Best for a Sporting Chance
Payne and Gunter

Mayfair House, Bellevue Road, Northolt, Middlesex. Tel (0181) 842 2224

So you want to watch the racing, go golfing and try the rugby? Payne and Gunter are your corporate entertainers. They've been at it for over 200 years and are the Godzillas of the catering world. They are experienced in shifting tons of cutlery, china, marquees and, inevitably, portaloos, all over the country. What they don't know about the insides of Hampton Court, Syon House and Goodwood isn't worth printing.

Party Shops

If you're going to have a party you might as well do it right. It doesn't matter how old you are, everyone expects a party hat, a streamer, bunting and that mandatory going-home present. Stepping into a party shop is the chance to regress to childhood and rediscover those early-life novelties. Yes, among many other childhood favourites, they still make those wonderful twirly straws which make an infuriating noise when blown – no party is complete without them!

Best for Balloons

Just Balloons

127 Wilton Road, SW1.Tel (0171) 434 3039

As the name suggests, this shop is balloon-mad, with every shape and colour in stock. Fancy a balloon made up in the shape of a Champagne bottle, or a frog? A single foil balloon, without a message, costs £2.50; with a message, £2.75. They sell other things, too, such as paper plates, party poppers and crackers, and, if you buy a gift as well as a balloon they will deliver to your door. A hand-delivered balloon with a personalised message costs from £21.15 including VAT.

Best for Christmas

Christmas Shop

Hays Galleria, 55a Tooley Street, SE1. Tel (0171) 378 1998

They quite literally celebrate Christmas all year round at the Christmas Shop. Fancy decorating a Christmas tree in June? Well, provided you are prepared to settle for an artificial tree and you're not expecting a real one in June, you will not be disappointed. In order not to alienate their non-Christmas customers throughout the year, they also stock a general selection of party goods and cards. Mail order is also available.

Best for Non-stop Partying

Non-stop Party Shop

214-216 Kensington High Street, W8. Tel (0171) 937 7200

You can buy everything here from fancy dress to bouncy castles – the list is endless. Walk in looking for one thing and you will be sure to leave with ten others. This place is enormous fun and items are displayed in ways that encourage you to spend hours gawping. Many products can be hired, including 'number' cake tins and children's portable tables and chairs. Seasonal party costumes make for a constantly changing window display.

Best for Stars and Stripes

American Party Store

16 Woodstock Street, W1. Tel (0171) 493 2678

To make someone feel special at their party, it's hard to beat personalised decorations. This American store does a great line in customising paper decorations. It takes about a week to do, but the results are spectacular. They import their novelties from America, so you can expect surprises such as Punch starter kits and an all-American cookie jar. They also have a balloon delivery and cake-making service.

Best Tried-and-Tested

Barnum's

67 Hammersmith Road, W14. Tel (0171) 602 1211

These people have been doing roaring business for years providing a great service covering most party knick-knacks, such as bunting, masks, fake moustaches, and balloons. Great for fancy dress party accessories, too. You will be surrounded by people screaming with laughter in the shop as they try on fake noses and glasses.

Party Venues

Sometimes your drawing room will not hold the horde of friends you want with you to celebrate momentous occasions in your life. A little research could find you at your next party singing Happy Birthday to a hippo or gliding along the Thames by moonlight.

Best for Dramatic Backdrops
The Natural History Museum

Cromwell Road, South Kensington, SW7. Tel (0171) 938 9123

Have you ever fancied sharing your party with a Dinosaur? Give your friends an education when you hire this museum for your dance or cocktail party. Book early though – this venue has been housing all kinds of revelry for the past 10 years and its popularity is growing all the time. To rent the Hall until one in the morning costs £6,600; the museum will suggest caterers, lighting schemes, and entertainers.

Best for Children
London Zoo

Regents park, NW1. Te (0171) 586 4112

Children parties can be a nightmare. There is always one child who eats too much jelly and another who is intent on sending at least one to hospital. Here in the banqueting suites they can tuck into a child-friendly menu whilst wearing animal masks. Menus cost from £12–£13 per head and a cake can be organised as well as entertainers.

Best for Wannabees
Hampton Court Palace
East Molesey, Surrey. Tel (0181) 781 9500

Be Henry VIII's seventh wife and hold your party in the Tudor apartments. Have a small sit-down dinner for four hundred or a reception in the Great Hall. No candlelight or furtive cigarette-smoking behind the curtains is permitted – the management is justifiably paranoid since the fire in 1986. Caterers and entertainers can be suggested and for those who want something that little different, you can rent the Garden Café or have a 1920's style wedding reception.

Best for Wedding Parties
Royal Geographic Society
1 Kensington Gore, Kensington, SW7. Tel (0171) 589 5466

If you are holding your wedding reception in London but want that country feel, this is the place for you. Their wild gardens are very popular for wedding guests who have had one too many glasses of champagne. The Main Hall, New Map Room and The Tea Room can be hired for £150 an hour and will hold up to 360 people. Lodge Caterers are on hand for various delicious nibbles and marquees can be erected in the garden for the unpredictable British weather.

Best for Rocking Parties
The Floating Boater
1 Bishops Bridge Road, Little Venice, W2. Tel (0171) 724 8740

For those who want a trip up the river, The Floating Boater will cruise you through Regents Park, by London Zoo and up to Camden. They can accommodate up to 100 people, and up to 50 for a sit-down dinner. It costs £160 an hour with a minimum two-hour charter and they will provide a live band or disco.

Personal Fitness Trainers

Feeling sluggish? Are those rolls of fat still wobbling minutes after you have sat down? For some, exercise is a passion and for others it is about as realistic a prospect as a trip to the moon. These days, a fitness trainer is not exclusive to those with a record or movie deal or those with fat wads of cash. You can be made to run for miles, lift weights and sweat like a pig under the careful instruction of your very own trainer.

Best for Fun

Peter Stephens

Tel (0181) 894 9876 or (0973) 316 955

Peter Stephens will make you laugh as you sweat your way to fitness. He once played Puck in a Royal Shakespeare Company production of A Midsummer Night's Dream and his lively personality will either encourage or antagonise you into trying harder. He concentrates mostly on the aerobic side of fitness and is a great exponent of the humble step. An hour's session with him costs £30.

Best for Royal Workouts

Doreen Whittaker

Tel (0181) 840 6260; c/o The Harbour Club, Water Meadow Lane, SW6. Tel (0171) 371 7700

Are you a middle-aged wobbler envious of Princess Diana's sleek figure? Then Doreen Whittaker, responsible for Di's toned physique, is the person to see. She fits her personal training sessions around her job as studio manager and seems to have a never-ending supply of energy as she bounces from person to person. Her intense workouts are mainly cardiovascular and are held in the gym or in the nearby park. If you think one session a week will satisfy Ms Whittaker then you are mistaken, as she recommends participation in other sports as well. She will take on anyone, including those of us classified as lost causes. Most book her for three sessions a week and pay £40 an hour.

Best for Pregnant Women
Amanda Kitchen

Tel (0181) 549 2744

Unfortunately we women are not made of elastic. After giving birth we don't suddenly spring back into shape. So along with dealing with a hysterical baby that keeps us awake all day and night we are expected to exercise our way back to our previous svelte selves. Amanda Kitchen is specially qualified to look after expectant and new mothers. Under her instruction saggy tummy muscles will be a thing of the past and people will stop asking you when you are expecting your next baby. Prices are around £30 an hour.

Best On Wheels
Pia Ingvarsson

Tel (0181) 788 5507

If gyms bring you out in a rash then Pia Ingvarsson has the perfect solution. You can be the focus of attention as you tumble and wobble your way through Richmond Park and Kensington Gardens on a pair of rollerblades. Pia Ingvarsson coaxes and coaches her clients until, without realising it, they actually start to get fit. For those worried about developing thunder thighs and tree-trunk legs Pia assures us that, in fact, 'it's so slimming for the legs.' She charges £35 an hour.

Personal Shoppers

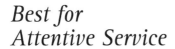

If you don't have time to dash from shop to shop or are simply clueless about what to buy, or what colours suit you, these are the people to call for a stress-free shopping experience.

Best for Attentive Service

Selfridges

400 Oxford Street, W1. Tel (0171) 318 3536

Gabriella di Nora eats, sleeps and breathes her job and is always on hand to help. She and her staff of seven will visit you at home or in the shop so that they can learn what you like and dislike. Clothes can be delivered to your home to try on and you can keep them overnight with no obligation to buy. The service is free of charge and there is also a free giftwrapping service.

Best for Insight

Wardrobe

42 Conduit Street, W1. Tel (0171) 494 1131

Susie Faux has been helping people to dress for work for 20 years. She has an expert eye for middle-age spread – the straining button on a man's jacket and the tight skirt across a woman's behind – and is there to transform her clients and ensure they turn other people's heads again.

Best for a Male Opinion
Harvey Nichols

109-125 Knightsbridge, SW1. Tel (0171) 235 5000

Harvey Nichols was the pioneer behind personal shopping and now serves its customers in a separate suite. Personal Shopper Boris Zbikowski believes that women like having him as their guide because, he says, men are more honest! The service is free of charge and includes changing facilities and showers.

Best for Men
Malcolm Levene

13-15 Chiltern Street, W1. Tel (0171) 487 4383

Some men are hopeless at shopping and have no patience for it. Realising this, the staff at this retail shop take their male customers under their wing and help them to make the right decisions. There is no obligation to buy and you can even bring in your own fabric to have made up as a suit. Malcolm Levene is hot property and now works part-time here and in LA. Don't worry if he is abroad, Grant Boston, who has been the stylist for New Order and Issey Miyake, is his right-hand man.

Best for the Right Colour
Colour Me Beautiful

59 & 66 Abbey Business Centre, Ingate Place, SW8. Tel (0171) 627 5211

Do you look sick in yellow and washed out in black? The staff here help you to realise your potential through colours that suit you best. If this sounds like a hangover from the 80 s, it is, but the philosophy is that the hue you wear can bear a strong influence on how others perceive you. They note your skin and eye colouring and then drape certain colours over your shoulders. The service costs £55. If you take their advice, you will no longer clash with your clothes.

Pet Shops

No other country loves its animals as much as the British and increasingly, it is not just cats and dogs people want to cuddle up to. Exotica such as tarantulas and terrapins are the companion of choice. Almost anything is available, and nothing is more than a tube ride away.

Best for Accessories
Petworld

163–165 Bromley Road, Catford, SE6. Tel (0181) 698 1232; and Units 1–3, Broadway Retail Park, off Cricklewood Lane, NW2

Petworld proudly calls itself 'Europe's Finest Pet Store'. Dogs and cats are catered for, but you can also buy food for rabbits, birds, hamsters and almost any animal imaginable. Also available are toys and scratching posts for cats and playhouses for hamsters. Wisely, after all the excitement, urine-absorber is also on sale.

Best for Aftercare
Pets' Place

105 Central Road, Worcester Park, Surrey. Tel (0181) 296 0444

Ian Veal, manager at Pets' Place, is concerned with sick animals. "Often, people can't afford vets' fees", he explains, "and frequently remedies can be bought cheaper from the shelves". He believes that many dogs' problems are due to using the wrong kind of food, and recommends 'wholefoods' such as Eukanuba and Hill's Science Diet.

Best for Exotica
Regent Pet Centre

35–37 Parkway, NW1. Tel (0171) 284 0730

Barry Hales's Establishment opened in 1918, and has, in the past, provided customers with lions, tigers and dozens of chimps. Nowadays, however, they specialise in exotic birds (all of which are bred in this country), amphibians and spiders of all species. Spiders range in price from £10–100. Simon King, resident expert, told us that he is not allowed to sell anything venomous, with the sole exception of tarantulas, whose bite has been compared to a bee sting. Also available are a pair of hyacinth macaws... if you have £30,000 or so to spare.

Best for Grand Pets

Animal Fair

17 Abingdon Road, W8. Tel (0171) 937 0011

This pet shop is one of the smartest in central London, where there are precious few. Patrons include dowagers, dukes, lords and ladies by the score, not to mention countless other residents of the Royal Borough. Animal Fair does a good line in week-end boarding for small animals such as gerbils, rabbits and mice, at about £2.00 a day. They also provide a grooming service, as well as accessories, coats and combs, etc.

Best for Variety

Pet City

Imperial Retail Park, Thames Way, Gravesend, Kent. Tel (01474) 534 475;
St James Retail Park, Edinburgh Way, Harlow, Essex. Tel (01279) 443 613

This chain of pet stores is billed as the biggest in Europe with 31 branches all over the country and more due to open in central London later this year. Over 9,000 products are on sale at these stores and a wide range of animals is available, including spiders, hampsters, mice and gerbils. It seems strange, however, that there seems to be a curious lack of dogs and cats available, since we all know they are the most popular pets in Britain.

Photographic Developers

The holiday is over and all that you have left, apart from a fading tan, is a roll of film filled with snaps of your holiday romance. The question is where is the best place in London to get these photo-opportunities developed? Like everything in London, there are many ways to get the job done.

Best for Black And White

Sky Photographic Services

Ramillies House, 1-2 Ramillies Street, W1. Tel (0171) 434 2266

There are three other branches in Canon Street, Holborn, and Hackney. They all offer a wide range of photographic services, but they are best known for their black-and- white prints which are offered at competitive prices. It is possible to send your film and cheque by post, but it is advisable to call first to check the price. Black-and-white prints, 7in by 5in, cost £3 each plus VAT.

Best for Enlargements

Fotostop Express

109 High Street, Penge, SE20. Tel (0181) 776 8139

This is the place to come to get your photographs reprinted, enlarged or duplicated. An 8in by 12in enlargement, including a mount, will set you back £2.50, while two sets of prints of a 36-exposure 35mm film will cost £4.99. A black- and-white service is available, but it takes up to a week.

Best for Photographic Novelties

Boots

127A High Street Kensington, W8. Tel (0171) 937 9533

If you are bored with straightforward photographs, there is no better place to go than inside the familiar portals of Boots the Chemist. Boots offers a whole range of novel ways in which to present your family snaps and jokey moments. For £8, it will splash your pictures across a jigsaw puzzle so that you can take them apart and put them together again at will. For £8, you can have a coaster made up displaying a loved (or not-so-loved) one or for £7.50, they will put a picture on the side of a mug.

Best for Professional Service

Joe's Basement

113-117 Wardour Street, W1. Tel (0171) 434 9313

In addition to the address given above, there is another branch of this famous photographic developers in the City. Both branches offer a wide range of services that are not normally available in high street branches, such as enhancements, sizes and contrasts. Their specialist service includes colour exhibition printing and master print variants. They also have a trade counter that is open 24 hours a day, 7 days a week which provides film from Fuji, Polaroid, and Kodak.

Picnic Caterers

Sometimes, come rain or shine, a picnic is the best choice for an intimate occasion or a party. If you can't face the prospect of making the sandwiches or cheese straws yourself, why not rely on the expertise of picnic caterers? At nearly one-third off the cost of eating in a swanky restaurant and being condescended to by arrogant waiters, there is no better way to spend the day than eating al fresco in one of London's beautiful parks – you can even bring the dog!

Best for Flexibility
Anna Fryer Catering

134 Lots Road, SW10. Tel (0171) 351 4333

Anna Fryer Catering will cope with any picnic idea that comes into your head. Prices range from between £12.50 to £40 per head and the food arrives in wicker baskets with paper plates or Crown Derby and crystal, depending on how glamorous you are feeling. Forty-eight hours' notice is required to rustle up delights such as lemongrass and crab tartlets, char-grilled fillet of salmon and couscous salad.

Best for Swank
Harrods

Knightsbridge, SW1. Tel (0171) 730 1234 ext. 2058/3552

If you want to have a picnic in real style, then Harrods is the place for you. Given forty-eight hours notice, the head chef will conjure up a veritable feast, including, among other delicious things, smoked salmon and duck. Your edible goodies will be presented in one of the store's gift boxes. Wicker baskets can also be hired for a deposit of £80 for two people.

Best for Themed Ideas
New Quebec Cuisine
13 New Quebec Street, W1. Tel (0171) 723 0128

Sharon Davy's innovative ideas are very well planned and executed. Her naughty-but-nice picnics arrange for you to be carried to the picnic site in a white Cadillac convertible with the registration number 2BONK. She needs forty-eight hours notice to get the whole package together and her insulated hamper boxes cost from £25 per person. Entertainment is also available to order.

Best for Traditional Style
Fortnum & Mason
Piccadilly, W1. Tel (0171) 734 8040

Given the standard 48 hours notice, there is a wide range of fresh picnic selections available, starting at around £25 and going up to £110. Picnics in the higher price range are produced in a wicker basket for £100 deposit. You can also create your own picnic from the 'Traiteur' menu which includes asparagus and lobster.

Best for Unusual Requests
The Pie Man Catering Company
23 Pensbury Street, SW8. Tel (0171) 627 5232

This place puts the glitz into your picnic by providing such luxuries as butlers, garden furniture, and chauffeur-driven cars. A mini marquee for two with a Scots piper was one strange request they coped with. The food is delicious and ranges in price from £15–£25 per head. Forty-eight hours notice is required to create a feast. Expect to tuck into mouth-watering delights such as sun-dried tomato and pesto roulade.

Picture Restorers

They say every picture is worth a thousand words, and some are worth a lot more than that. Whether, like the Yellow Pages commercial, someone has drawn glasses on your Mum's portrait or drunken Uncle Tom, after one too many, has poked his finger through the Constable, help is at hand.

Best for Oil Paintings

Diana Reeves

24 Applegarth Road, W14. Tel (0171) 603 8603

Diana Reeves has 25 years' experience and specialises in all ages of oil paintings on canvas and panels. Diana recently worked on a badly-restored portrait of Queen Anne which she brought to life again for £800. Her prices start at £150. For a charge, she also does home inspections and collections and deliveries.

Best for Old-established

Drown and Company

117 Boundary Road, NW8. Tel (0171) 624 6100

This family business, founded in 1888, specialises in all types of paintings, but is particularly good with Impressionist and Modern. Simple surface cleaning starts at around £30, but rectifying inexpert restoration can push the price up somewhat. David Drown, the former chairman of the ABPR (Association of British Picture Restorers), advises people to get several quotes before deciding on a restorer for the job. 'It's not unknown,' he says, 'for prices to vary by hundreds of pounds.'

Best for Prints

Sheila Fairbrass and Keith Holmes

27 Dalebury Road, SW17. Tel (0181) 672 4606

These two work together under the same roof but they tackle very different things. Sheila Fairbrass specialises in modern works of art on paper while Keith Holmes will take up the challenge to try his hand at anything on paper. They have restored mildewed 19th-century hunting prints for between £35 and £50.

Best for Service

J.H. Cooke & Son

Station Avenue, Kew, Surrey. Tel (0181) 940 5188

Philip and Michael Robinson, fellows of the ABPR, and Janet Robinson run this company in Mayfair. Started in the 1920s, it specialises in oil paintings and offers home inspections and free estimates. If you live in Central and West London they also offer a free collection and delivery service. Repairing, relining and cleaning a 17in by 22in Victorian flower painting, for example, costs from £400.

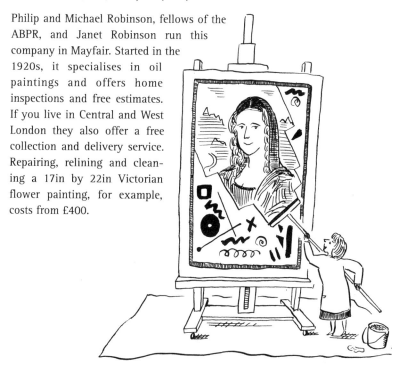

Places to Begin a Romance

Wouldn't you know it? Right out of the blue you find yourself embarking on a new romance and you have no idea how it sprung up on you. If that is the case it is very important to get the location right. Why risk everything unless you can do it in style with a bit of excitement? Most hotels offer rooms for the afternoon – ostensibly to shower, change and rest – at half rates. And there are a lot of public places where you can kindle and keep the spark of love alive.

Best for Good Food

Hyde Park Hotel

66 Knightsbridge, SW1X 7JX. Tel (0171) 235 2000

Deep in the heart of Knightsbridge, the Hyde Park Hotel offers afternoon rates for £100 (lunchtime till 6pm). What could be a better way of spending an afternoon than sampling a delicious lunch at the restaurant, run by Marco Pierre White, followed by a leisurely 'rest' in one of rooms upstairs? And if things get too leisurely there is always the lingerie department at Harvey Nichols, over the road, to perk up proceedings.

Best Place To Propose

The Whispering Gallery

St Paul's Cathedral, EC4

What exactly you propose in this romantic setting is irrelevant, but if being overheard really turns you on, this could be the just the place for you. On the other hand, if you believe there is no passion without pain, you could try the Stone Gallery with its outside benches and telescopes. Or if you're a real glutton for punishment, the 530 steps to the Golden Gallery might spice things up a little bit.

Best for Sheer Luxury

The Ritz Hotel

Piccadilly, W1V OBR. Tel (0171) 794 0240

A lazy walk through St James's Park, head resting on your lover's shoulder, feeding the ducks, followed by a refreshing glass of Champagne before dining in the belle-époque splendour of the Ritz's Louis XVI restaurant. Sounds like bliss? Well, it's not just for the Lauren Bacalls of this world.

Best for Value

Richmond Park

Surrey

A beautiful spring day, eating alfresco with the one you love, is hard to beat. Buy a decent bottle of wine, read some good poetry, concoct a picnic of breathtaking delicacies and lose yourselves in bracken, woods, deer and foxes for the day. But remember to take a rug – and to pick the leaves out of your hair before returning to where you should really be!

Best for Watching Films

Prince Charles Cinema

Leicester Place, WC2 H7BP. Tel (0171) 494 4687

Maybe time is not on your side or you just like watching a good old romantic black-and-white film with the one you love. The seats at this cinema do not have any arm rests so who knows what ending you will find here.

Places to Sleep Rough

It's not always necessary to pay out extortionate amounts for a hotel when one simply cannot afford it or has lost the where-with-all. There are plenty of places in London where you can grab forty winks if you are crafty enough to find them – and cunning enough to remain inconspicuous.

Best for After the Party
The Albert Hall
Kensington Gore, SW7

Astounding as it may seem, the Albert Hall has been known to house the odd stray for the night after late-night revelling at a charity ball or dance. Such people have discovered that, before the night is through and the music is about to strike up the final strains, it's a good idea to bolt down to the musician's dressing-rooms (usually unattended on these occasions) and snuggle down on one of the benches to be found there. Then, after daybreak, when the place comes to life, they sneak out through one of the doors (hopefully) unnoticed. Mind you, it takes a brave person to stagger through Central London still in a ball gown/black tie in broad daylight in pursuit of transport.

Best for an All-round Experience
The Circle Line
London Transport

If you have been out on the town all night, having told your wife or husband that you would only be stopping for a 'quick drink after work', the Circle Line might be the answer before returning home to face the music. It usually opens around 5am and for the price of a one-stop ticket you can travel round and round in relative warmth and comfort until you have thought up a good excuse. A few hours on the tube is also guaranteed to give the tell-tale signs of scent or aftershave enough time to evaporate (although you may prefer this smell to the one that will undoubtedly linger in its place).

Best for a Bargain

Le Meridien Piccadilly

Piccadilly, W1. Tel (0171) 734 8000

Although by no stretch of the imagination could this hotel in the heart of London be considered a place for slumming, it could be a god-send if you are used to the good life but find yourself temporarily short of funds. The trick is to go down to the Burlington Bar in the basement and nurse a drink till 1am. After this time, rooms that have been booked by customers through Am/Ex and who have failed to turn up get given away at a huge discount.

Best for Media Types

The Groucho Club

44 Dean Street, W1. Tel (0171) 439 4685

Sometimes after a long lunch it's just not conducive to return to the office before meeting the boss for an update on that latest report. A little snooze can work wonders. So if you can sneak into the Groucho Club and find the members' television room upstairs you'll find plenty of comfortable sleeping posts to while away the afternoon. One lady recently managed to snore for four solid hours without interruption.

Present Shops

Giving presents is supposed to be an easy, fun thing to do. In an ideal world we should be able to give someone something as simple as a Mars bar and bask in the reflected glory. But, unfortunately, life can be a bit more difficult than that and buying presents can be a real headache. These one-stop present shops claim to be the solution.

Best for a Distinctive Print
Liberty
210-221 Regent Street, W1. Tel (0171) 734 1234

This is definitely a first stop in the search for presents. Liberty might seem a bit too flowery at times, but it has an enviable selection of china and glass and a newly revamped perfume section. Household designer objects can be found in abundance and, whatever you do, don't miss the jewellery department.

Best for Home Stuff
Habitat
208-222 Kings Road, SW3 and branches. Tel (0171) 351 1211

This is a wonderful place for finding great things for a person's home, from toothmugs, candlesticks and brightly coloured pasta bowls to sofas and coffee tables. The Habitat style is simple so, even if you have no taste at all, you cannot go wrong.

Best for Lefties
Anything Left-handed
57 Brewer Street, W1. Tel (0171) 437 3910

There are great presents to be found at this shop for poor, unfortunate, left-handed friends who usually suffer in silence while others look on in ignorance of the efforts they are making. Here you can buy left-handed can openers and scissors, anti-clockwise clocks, boomerangs and books. And for the left-handed boozer a very handy corkscrew is one of the shop's best sellers. There is also an excellent children's section.

Best for Little Silver Things
Finishing Touch

197 New King's Road, SW6. Tel (0171) 736 0410

Because everything here looks such good quality it is easy to be deceived into thinking that it is all very expensive. Actually, most things in this shop are very reasonable and weekday about-towners come here in droves to kit themselves and their friends out with bags, scarves and little silver things to take back to the country at the weekend.

Best for Times Gone By
Past Times

102 Kings Road, SW3. Tel (0171) 591 0068
146 Brompton Road, SW3. Tel (0171) 581 7616
155 Regent Street, W1. Tel (0171) 734 3728
179 Kensington High Street, W8. Tel (0171) 795 6344

A mecca for nostalgic shoppers and admirers of craft work from years gone by, these shops are sectioned into various stages of history, from the Middle Ages to Victorian times and beyond. There are games and jewellery as well as an assortment of knick-knacks, which make perfect stocking fillers. Take care, it is all too easy to overlook lovely things in this shop and it is well worth taking time for a second look.

Private Dining Rooms

If you can't bear the idea of cooking an elaborate meal for masses of guests but, equally, don't like the thought of being in a noisy restaurant, then what about hiring your own private dining room?

Best for Heads of State and Captains of Industry

The Trafalgar Suite at the Ritz

Piccadilly, W1. Tel (0171) 493 8181

The Trafalgar Suite at the Ritz Hotel is the place to brush up on your knowledge of foreign politicians. Visitors have included such famous Heads of State as Gorbachev, Mitterand and Kohl, and people return over and over again for the unbeatable service. The Suite seats up to 20 people and has incredible views over Green Park. The menu starts from £40.

Best River View

The Pinafore Room

Savoy Hotel, WC2. Tel (0171) 836 4343

This room not only has a wonderful view, but a delightful tale to go with it. The unfortunate host of a dinner party for thirteen guests here back in the 19th century was found dead a week later. So nowadays if only thirteen guests pitch up to dinner, a 3ft-tall cat called Kaspar is produced. He wears a napkin around his neck, is brought a fresh bowl of milk for every course, and is quite a conversation piece.

Best for Rock Stars

Julie's

135 Portland Road, W11. Tel (0171) 229 8331

The Rolling Stones and Guns 'n Roses are among the many rock stars who have thrown wild parties here since its opening in 1969. The room is also popular for stag nights – Mark Philips held his here and the occasion is commemorated by a stag's head on the wall. It was also Prince Charles's first choice, but at the last moment word got out and the venue had to be changed. The room seats 26; menu from £20.

Best to See and Be Seen

Quaglino's

16 Bury Street, SW1. Tel (0171) 930 6767

If you want to get away from the hustle-and-bustle of a restaurant, but want to see and be seen, this is the place for you. The private dining room is above the kitchen overlooking the main dining room. If you want more privacy, then the curtains can be lowered over the wall of glass. The room seats up to 40. The menu is around £20 for lunch and £30 for the evening.

Best for Theatreland

The Ivy

1 West Street, WC2. Tel (0171) 836 4751

The Ivy's private dining room has the same look as the main restaurant and seats up to 60 people. Actors and media moguls alike have been entertained here for first- and last-night parties as well as various launches. The menu starts at £21.50.

Psychotherapists

*The British are renowned for thinking they are 'above'
therapy and for believing this is a fashionable quirk indulged
in by Americans. Then again, the British are also renowned
for not facing up to their problems!*

Best for Bioenergetics
The Bioenergetic Partnership

22 Fitzjohns Avenue, NW3. Tel (0171) 435 1079

Don't be fooled by the name – this is not some new yoghurt product!
Bioenergetics is a therapy which states that emotional problems can
be manifested in physical tensions. The people who come here are
usually those who feel that other therapies have not helped them; or
those who are either inarticulate or too articulate. The cost is £25 for
one session and both group and individual sessions are available.

Best for Freudian Psychoanalysis
The Institute of Psychoanalysis

63 New Cavendish Street, W1. Tel (0171) 580 4952

The therapy here digs deep into childhood memories you might prefer
to forget. The theory is that if you relive nightmare relationships
then you will be able to understand and let go of the neurotic disaster
you have become. To make an appointment, call (0171) 436 1177.
They will assess you, then refer you to a psychoanalyst. £25 upwards

Best for Gestalt Therapy
The Gestalt Centre

64 Warwick Road, St Albans, Herts. Tel (01727) 864806

There is no hiding in the closet here. The idea, using imagery and
your dreams, is to make you take control of your life and stand on
your own two feet. Ideal for anyone who is experiencing a sexual

lull or marital difficulties – anything, in fact, to do with the complex make-up of 1990s' relationships. The Gestalt Centre will put you in touch with therapists and the cost per session is from £25. This price is reduced if you make an appointment with a final-year trainee.

Best for Jungian Analysis
The Society Of Analytical Psychology

1 Daleham Gardens, NW3. Tel (0171) 435 7696

Have you ever wanted to know what that dream meant when you ran down the street stark naked and no one batted an eyelid? Well, this place could provide the answer. They focus on the present rather than the past and take an interest in your dreams as well as your fantasies. This is an ideal place for people who are trying to deal with a trauma or are contemplating the meaning of life. The therapy is long-term and you will be assessed before being handed over to a therapist. The cost is £20 to £40 a session, but low-cost therapy is also available.

Best for Psychosynthesis
The Institute Of Psychosynthesis

65A Watford way, NW4. Tel (0181) 202 4525

The approach taken by the Institute of Psychosynthesis combines eastern and western philosophies, and is perfect for those on a quest to find themselves. The fact that you might be a neurotic person is seen in context with your spiritual growth, and imagery and meditation is used. The weekly sessions cost £20 to £35 an hour, with the option of receiving low-cost therapy from trainees.

Restaurants For Children

When it comes to taking children out for a meal, London still hasn't got it quite right. Even though parents are no longer entirely limited to grotty burger and fish bars, we still have a lot to learn from our Continental friends who welcome children with open arms to nearly all establishments – believing they actually enhance the place.

Best for Entertainment
Sol e Luna
22 Shorts Garden, WC2. Tel (0171) 379 3336

Where children are concerned, you can never fail with a good old standby pizza. Here, along with this finger-food, there is also Spotty Dotty on hand to entertain the kids between 1pm and 3 pm. The kids' menu, which includes pizza, pasta, and ice-cream, costs £3.95. Adults eat a similar menu but have the additional choice of grills for between £8 to £10. Open Sunday from noon to 10.30 pm.

Best for Parents
Chiaroscuro
24 Coptic Street, WC1. Tel (0171) 636 2731

The chef picks the adult menu while the chef's daughter chooses the children's menu. Chef Sally James cooks up delicious dishes such as a dolcelatte soufflé, chargrilled lamb, marinaded vegetables and couscous and serves it to the adults in the dining room. It's the children who get the choice of venue – with or without parents. They can, if they wish, eat in the playroom on a different floor from their parents. Open Sunday 11am–3pm.

Best for the Park

The Original Maids of Honour Restaurant

Kew Road, Richmond. Tel (0181) 940 2752

This popular restaurant sells kids' favourites at a reasonable price. Great fun for lunch or tea after exhausting the little darlings round the wonderful grounds of Kew. Babies are welcome. Get here early to avoid a long queue. Advisable to book. (Closed Sundays).

Best for All Ages

Smollensky's on the Strand

105 The Strand, WC2. Tel (0171) 497 2101

This is definitely a kids' outing that combines food and entertainment. There is a play area for the under-sevens, magic shows, and clowns and magicians wandering around. For kids who think they are too old for this kind of thing, there is a Gameboy and Nintendo on hand to keep them happy. The food is mainly American and is reasonably priced. A main course for a child costs £3.99; for adults it works out at about £15 without drink. Open Sunday noon–5.30pm.

Riding Lessons

After watching International Velvet innumerable times, riding can look easy, but it's not! London riding stables coach kids, middle-aged wobblers and the totally uncoordinated. Although your muscles may never forgive you, there is nothing quite like cantering across wide spaces – as long as you manage to stay on!

Best for Adults
Wimbledon Village Stables
24 High Street, SW19. Tel (0181) 946 8579

This small informal stables has been teaching Londoners to ride for many years. Friendly instructors coax their charges into cantering and prancing about Wimbledon Common before they know what's hit them. Lessons cost from £14 to £25 and you are certain to find your very own Red Rum (or Dobbin, depending on your temperament) among the sixteen horses available. Organised trips to horse shows, two-hour rides and pub rides are also on offer.

Best for Boarding Horses
Aldersbrook Riding School & Livery Yard
Empress Avenue, E12. Tel (0181) 530 4648

No matter how much your roses would enjoy the manure, you can't really keep a horse in the garden of a terraced house. From £45 a week you can, however, keep your horse at Aldersbrook Riding School. Your horse need never be lonely here, as he or she will have another 35 horses for company. If you just want to learn to ride, or canter through nearby Epping Forest, a half-hour lesson will cost you £11.

Best for the Competitor-to-Be
Belmont Riding Centre
The Ridgeway, NW7. Tel (0181) 906 1255

This centre has access to 150 acres of land in Mill Hill. They are lucky enough to have a cross-country course and are known to be good for training people up to hunting and competition standard. As they are further from the centre of London, they are cheaper than the other stables listed here. An hour's group lesson costs £13.50; a private lesson £19.

Best for Well-heeled Riders
Hyde Park Stables
63 Bathurst Mews, W2. Tel (0171) 723 2813

An hour's riding lesson here costs £28 for a group, and £60 for a private lesson. These relatively high prices are compensated for by a ride through Hyde Park. The stables specialise in both children and adults and will take on anyone from an absolute beginner to a know-it-all.

Best for Miles
Kingston Riding Centre
38 Crescent Road, Kingston, Surrey. Tel (0181) 546 6361

If cantering through the park with the wind flying through your hair is your cup of tea, then Richmond's 2,400 acres of woodland and the breath-taking views of the Thames Valley are ideal spots for horsey activities. Kingston Riding Centre will get you up to speed in their own school before setting you loose in the park either with an instructor or in groups.

School Accessories

Going back to school can be more of a trauma for little Johnny than some parents realise. If your child doesn't have a Pocahontas writing set or the Power Rangers pencil sharpener, then he or she can be relegated to the ranks of a nerd for the rest of his or her school career. And where do you go to get the hated uniform and the dreaded beginning-of-term haricut?

Best for Books

The Children's Bookshop

29 Fortis Green Road, N10. Tel (0181) 444 5500

This inspirational shop will entice even the most reluctant reader. In years to come, your offspring may be among the many visitors who come back to see the owner, Helen Paiba, to announce that they are now a high-flying English graduate. If a book is not stocked, they will order it especially for you. The shop is filled with reading-scheme books, dictionaries, bibles and atlases, as well as language and geography books.

Best for Haircuts
Trotters
34 King's Road, SW3. Tel (0171) 259 9620

Come here to give your child the ultimate back-to-school accessory – a haircut to show off in the playground. Trotters promises a non-crying experience and those who behave get a handful of Smarties as a treat. Most kiddies sit quite calmly watching the fish tanks in front of them. Make sure you book beforehand – Trotters can do up to 50 haircuts a day in the back-to-school rush.

Best for Jokes
Oscar's Den
127-129 Abbey Road, NW6. Tel (0171) 328 6683

On the first day at a new school all children feel the need to make an impression. Ignore the fact that you are probably setting your child up for the first detention of the year and take him or her to Oscar's Den. This shop is filled with jokes and novelties for less than £2. Great first-day presents for the new teacher include an exploding pen and a collection of furry mice. For children at boarding school who run out of ammunition, there is a mail-order service

Best for School Uniforms
Marks & Spencer
All major stores

M&S school uniforms come in all shapes and sizes and are machine-washable. There are several styles of skirts, pinafores, shirts, blazers and trousers, including a wide range of hard-wearing shoes. The best thing about M&S is that you go in under the guise of doing some school-uniform shopping and end up spending a fortune on yourself!

Second-hand Record Shops

Are you still listening to your old record player while everyone else has leapt forward light years in technology? Or are you just looking for that certain record to remind you of your youth? Whatever the case, London is full of second-hand record shops to help you along – and to stop you from making expensive mistakes...

Best for a Bargain
Cheapo Cheapo Records

53 Rupert Street, W1. Tel (0171) 437 8272

As the name suggests, this is the best place to find extremely cheap and interesting records. Prices seem to have stood still while time races on, and you can pick up that record you have been searching for, for as little as £2.20. The possibilities are endless – this shop stocks anything that is vinyl and plays some sort of music.

Best for the Committed Collector
U.F.O

18 Hanway Street, W1. Tel (0171) 636 1281

This is the place where serious buyers come to supplement their record collections, but it doesn't come cheap. For example, a rare Beatles' LP with the 'Butcher' cover will set you back £500. Along with the records there is a collection of autographs and pictures to send die-hard fans into a swoon. For those looking for something a bit more modern and not so expensive, head dowstairs, where you will find a wide range of records including new-wave and rock.

Best for Jazz

Ray's Jazz Shop

180 Shaftesbury Avenue, WC2. Tel (0171) 240 3969

This friendly store has a constant flow of eager customers snapping up its vinyl. Unlike the rest of the world, it has tried to stay away from the CD. There are lots of good-value second-hand and new records and you'll find anything from New Orleans to modern avant-garde. Downstairs there is a not-to-be-missed blues section.

Best for US Independents

Intoxica!

231 Portobello Road, W11.Tel (0171) 229 8010

This shop on the Portobello road has a wide range of second-hand jazz, soundtracks, exotica, soul, and records from the 1960s, plus facilities for you to listen before you buy. The basement has been taken over by US independents and dance music, and there is a catalogue available for the new records.

Best for the Record Watcher

Reckless Records

30 Berwick Street, W1. Tel (0171) 437 4271
79 Upper Street, N1. Tel (0171) 359 2222

The longer a record stays in this shop the cheaper it gets, which probably explains why the starting prices are so high! You can find classical, reggae, jazz, country, rock and soul here. For the avid and committed collector the Upper Street branch of Reckless Records is well worth a look.

Security for the Home

There used to be a time when the only precaution Londoners took against burglars was a sign on the front door warning them to Beware Of The Dog - but that was back in the good old days along with The Smog and ration books. For the best and safest security in your home, use firms which are members of a relevant trade association. Names to look out for are MLA, the Master Locksmiths Association (01327 262 255), for an inspected member in your area, and NACOSS, National Approval Council for Security Systems, (01628 37512), for an approved member in your area.

Best for Starters

Phone your local police station for the local Metropolitan Police Crime Prevention Officer (CPO). Home security is a full-time job for specially trained CPOs, who will visit, free of charge, by appointment, to give a security survey. Expert advice on making your home as secure as possible, taking into account any individual or local problems.

Best One-stop Security Shop

Barry Bros

121-123 Praed Street, W2. Tel (0171) 723 9663

A showroom on two floors displays all the goods and services this flourishing family firm has to offer. Founded by Jack Barry in 1945, it is now run by his three sons. They have their own London-wide installation service for all types of locks, alarms, safes, grilles and security doors, employ their own fitters and are members of both MLA and NACOSS.

Best Lock-out

Banhams

233-235 Kensington High Street, W8. Tel (0171) 622 5151

Banhams is one of the oldest and best-known names in home security. W.F. Banham invented the first automatic door bolt in 1926 and founded the company of which his son Peter is chairman today. They make and install their own patented locks, and install other leading brands. They also supply and install security grilles, safes, entry telephones and alarms. So there is no need to call out the firebrigade if you're locked out at 3am as they have their own central monitoring service, with a unique 24-hour key holding service.

Best in Distress

Chiswick Security

4 Denbigh Street, SW1. Tel (0171) 630 6500
5 Chiswick Terrace, Acton Lane, W4. Tel (0181) 994 1474

Bob Efford and his two sons, Colin and Simon are 24-hour locksmiths and carpenters, with MLA and NACOSS membership. They will arrive within half an hour for lock-outs within the London area. Around fifty per cent of locks can be opened without damage, they say. Average call-out fee is £35 plus VAT or up to £55 plus VAT for a call-out during the night. Night-time calls are diverted to a director's home, who then alerts the duty locksmith.

Shaves

Women get to go to beauty parlours for luxurious makeovers, massages and sunbeds – but would a man dare to admit to wanting a facial? Your secret desire to be pampered can be respectably indulged with a shave at one of the following establishments.

Best for an Aristocratic Shave
Geo F. Trumper

9 Curzon Street, W1. Tel (0171) 499 1850. 20 Jermyn Street, SW1. Tel (0171) 734 6553. Simpson, Piccadilly, W1. Tel (0171) 734 2002 ext. 342

Time has stood still at this gentlemen's den, which opened in 1875. It's the sort of place to savour the moment and look around you as waistcoated barbers pander to your every whim – you could find yourself sitting next to John Major or Peter Ustinov. The rooms are decorated in turn-of-the-century wooden panelling. Trumper's stocks its own lotions and potions. A shave and hot towels costs £12.50

Best for Comfort
Michael at the Savoy

The Strand, WC2. Tel (0171) 379 3009

The atmosphere here is cosy and relaxed with simple décor. Michael tells us that the test of a good shave is being able to glide a playing card up and down your cheek. A shave with hot towels is £12.50.

Best for Entertainment
Daniel Rouah

7A Station Approach, Baker Street Station, NW1. Tel (0171) 487 3198

Television celebrity Daniel Rouah is known for his more than 100 television appearances and has papered his walls with publicity stills. Celebrity shaves include Lennox Lewis and Oliver Reed. And if you're clueless about how to shave, Daniel runs Monday night tutorials and telephone hot lines. A shave costs £14.50.

Best Long-standing

Taylor's of Old Bond Street

74 Jermyn Street, SW1. Tel (0171) 930 5544

This place was founded in 1854 and Leonard Taylor has four barbers shaving in his shop. The atmosphere is definitely gentlemen's club and Taylor's sells its own brand of scented shaving cream. A ten-minute massage with a shave is £19.90.

Best for Price

The Gentry

Ground Floor, Cabot Place West, E14. Tel (0171) 895 9929

This friendly shop is situated in Canary Wharf and has a fully operational chrome hot towel machine which has been converted to run off electricity. The unbeatable price of £8 for a shave is one that you won't want to miss.

Best for Tradition

Geoffrey's

9 Royal Exchange, Cornhill, EC3. Tel (0171) 626 7528

This family-run business has been going since 1934 and is situated near the Bank Of England. Tradition is the big word here and every-thing is old fashioned and to the point. £15 and 30 minutes later you will emerge feeling like a new man.

Shoe Shops

You can tell a lot about a person from their shoes. If you walk along the streets of London, you will see a lot of people wobbling, tottering and tripping up the road, but only a few who look really comfortable in their shoes. For the ultimate pair – whether you are into heels or flatties – try one of the shops listed here.

Best for DoctorMartins

Shellys

266-270 Regent Street, W1R 5DA. Tel (0171) 287 0939

As children reach their teenage years, getting a pair of shoes from Shellys is almost a rite of passage. Skinny legs are suddenly laced into Doctor Martin boots, never to come out again. You may curse the day you took your child there, but that is how Shellys finds its best customers. It grabs them when young and keeps them for many many years to come.

Best for Extravagance

Manolo Blahnik

49-51 Old Church Street, SW3. Tel (0171) 352 3863

Apart from revealing you as a woman of exquisite good taste, a pair of these shoes in your wardrobe is a real status symbol. They are so beautifully made that it is a question of finding a dress to match the shoes rather than shoes to match the dress! Prices start at about £230, but the purchase more than justifies the empty bank account and bare cupboards. Go on, splash out!

Best for Hand-made
Claire Norwood

404 St John Street, EC1. Tel (0171) 837 2355

To make your feet sing, why not have a pair of shoes hand-made especially for you? Customers of Claire Norwood enthuse about how comfortable the shoes are and how aching feet are a thing of the past. The price range is from £100 to £250, and the process of having your feet specially catered for takes up to six weeks. It may seem a long time, but the result is well worth the wait.

Best for Surprises
Savini

218 Upper Richmond Road, SW15. Tel (0181) 788 4537

Tucked away from those who pound the pavement of the Upper Richmond Road, is this jewel of a shoe shop. Savini has been run by owner Luciano Saviotti for ten years now. He is an incredible salesman who wants his customer to appreciate style and quality and, while you prance around trying on different styles, he will tell you their history. His beautiful shoes arrive from Italy and Spain every couple of months and are a steal from £20 to £70.

Best for Weddings
Emma Hope

33 Amwell Street, EC1R 1UR. Tel (0171) 833 2367

This is the place for your Big Day shoes. Emma Hope makes beautiful, strappy, head-turning numbers, which are perfect for summer. She does not limit herself to leather and suede, but creates shoes that fit like a glove from a linen/viscose knit. Her prices are around the £150 mark and the shoes will, without a doubt, take prime position in your wardrobe.

Short Courses

Your schooldays may be long gone, but that does not mean that your learning days are over. There are short courses available for a wide variety of subjects and there is usually something to please everybody, even children.

Best for Children's Pottery
Chelsea Pottery

5 Ebury Mews, SW1. Tel (0171) 259 0164

Ann James has been teaching children's ceramics for more than 20 years. She uses the Chelsea Pottery (founded 1952) as her home-from-home to pass on her skills to her protégés. 'Ann's classes are relaxed, happy, and flexible,' says director Richard Dennison. Classes are held on Saturday either in the morning or afternoon for £10 all inclusive. For budding adult potters, Wednesday is the night to sign up and get your hands dirty.

Best for Curtain-making
Judy St Johnston

46 Markham Street, SW3. Tel (0171) 352 2169

Not content with teaching pupils who listen to her every word in class, Judy St Johnston is now writing a book about curtain making. After a two-day course with her, your house will be transformed by beautiful curtains made by you. A second course will teach you how to add the frills. The cost of a course is £175.

Best for Decorative Paint Finishes
Hampstead Decorative Arts

2-20 Highgate High Street, N6. Tel (0181) 348 2811

This is where you can learn decorative paint effects to brighten the walls of your house, and you will not only keep up with, but surpass the Jones's. Harry Levinson left his career in film and television to tackle art on walls. He teaches everything from simple stippling to marbled and grained finishes. His three-day courses cost £165, including materials.

Best for Flower-arranging
Lady Pulbrooke Flower School

Liscartan House,127 Sloane Street, SW1. Tel (0171) 730 0030

In 1956 Lady Susan Pulbrooke set up her own flower shop with the aim of turning English country garden flowers into works of art. Recently, through teacher Susie Edwards, she set up her own flower-arranging school in London. The day-long course teaches basic skills such as arranging flowers for the home and church. The cost of the course is £145; this includes all materials as well as lunch.

Best for Stained Glass
Kate Baden Fuller

90 Greenwood Road, E8. Tel (0171) 249 0858

The skilled art of making stained glass could be yours for ever after just one two-day course with Kate Baden Fuller. Kate is an RCA-trained, stained-glass artist who was recently commissioned to tackle the senior common room at the South Bank University. All participants on Kate's course make their own stained-glass panel, using 12th-century techniques, which they can take home and show off to their friends once it is finished. The course costs £64 with an extra £14 for materials.

Specialist Libraries

Ordinary libraries are great for finding books about Tintin, or novels by Jilly Cooper, but if you need to find out more information for your thesis on Lenin, for example, you will need to visit a specialist library.

Best for Exclusivity

Marx Memorial Library

37-38 Clerkenwell Green, EC1. Tel (0171) 253 1485

You have to be a member to browse through the bookshelves here. There is an impressive collection of political literature, and when you are finished you can go and pay your respects to the library's namesake in Highgate cemetery. Open Monday to Friday 1pm-6pm, Saturday 10am-1pm. Closed Sundays.

Best for Going Back to School

University Of London Library

Senate House, Malet Street, WC2. Tel (0171) 636 4514

If you have a student ID, regardless of whether you went to school in South Dakota or Delhi, they will let you in. It doesn't come cheap for the eternally-broke student – £5 a day or £15 for a week. Inside are 1.5 million books on arts and humanities. Monday to Thursday 9.30am-9pm, Friday 9.30am-6pm, Saturday 9.30am-5.30pm.

Best for That Important Number
Westminster Central Reference Library

35 St Martin's Street, WC2. Tel (0171) 798 2034

With the use of the telephone directories housed in this reference library, you can phone anywhere in the world. The ground floor, which is only a small part of the building, includes an arts library, information on the performing arts and a list of companies trading in Britain. Open Monday–Friday 10am–7pm, Saturday 10am–7pm.

Best for Sound
National Sound Archive

29 Exhibition Road, SW7. Tel (0171) 412 7430

If there is a sound you want to assimilate, or if you simply want to sit down and listen to a book, this is the library for you. There is music from all times and countries, innumerable sound effects, wildlife noises and language tapes. You can spend all day plugged in listening to the sound of a loo flushing or learning how to introduce yourself in Chinese. No membership required. Open Monday to Friday 10am–5pm.

Best for Women's Issues
Feminist Library

5 Westminster Bridge Road, SE1. Tel (0171) 928 7789

Those who believe that women are under-represented in today's world will feel as if they have entered heaven when they find this place. Where women's issues are concerned, this is London's main library. It houses a resource centre filled to the brim with information, plus a large section of feminist fiction. Open Tuesday, 11am–8pm, Saturday and Sunday 2pm–5pm. Membership starts at £5.

Specialist Museums

The burning passions of the average punter cover a wide range of subjects. Some, believe it or not, are interested in blood and gore, others are obsessed with the challenge of sailing across the High Seas. These passions, and many others, are catered for by specialist museums.

Best for Those Called Watson
Sherlock Holmes Museum

221b Baker Street, NW1. Tel (0171) 935 8866

For years there was nothing to commemorate Sherlock Holmes, the detective to beat all others. But, for the past six years, his fans have been able to pay homage to their hero at this famous address in Baker Street. For super sleuths and fans of the books and films, there is more than ample memorabilia in the rooms to enable you to lose yourself in the special Sherlock Holmes atmosphere. Prices: adults £5, children £3.

Best for Pilots Of All Ages
Royal Air Force Museum

Grahame Park Way, Hendon, NW9. Tel (0181) 205 2266

Whatever your age, this is an incredible, unbeatable, visual experience. The Royal Airforce Museum is situated on an old airfield where you can see numerous aircrafts from the two World Wars, including the Sopworth Camel and the Lightning. There are also opportunities to experience, through a simulator, a flight in a Tornado and there are audio guides and a cinema. Prices: adults £5.20, children £2.60

Best for Government Secrets

Cabinet War Rooms

Clive Steps, King Charles St, SW1. Tel. (0171) 930 6961

While the 'ordinary' people hid in cellars during Second World War air-raids, those in Government ruled the country from the safety of the Cabinet War Rooms. Now it is possible to see into their world and wander through the Map Room, Cabinet Room and Transatlantic telephone rooms. Prices: adults £4, children £2.

Best for Those with Sea Legs

HMS Belfast

Morgan's Lane, Tooley Street, SE1. Tel (0171) 407 6434

HMS Belfast was launched as the biggest prize cruiser of the British Navy in 1938. Now it is a very popular seven-deck, floating naval museum, where you can get your sea legs and be transported into another world of punishment rooms and gun turrets. Prices: adults £4, children £2.

Best for Those with a Strong Stomach

Old St Thomas's Operating Theatre

9a St Thomas's Street, SE1. Tel (0171) 955 4791

This is not quite the London Dungeon, but it certainly captures the atmosphere of times past. This operating theatre, housed on the roof of St Thomas's Church, is the earliest of its kind. Set up to illustrate how it operated in the 19th century, it has most of its original furniture. For the squeamish, there are other exhibitions on display to divert attention from the gore. Prices: adults £2.50, children £1.20.

Tailors

Dissatisfied with department stores, and with endlessly looking for something that was obviously not made just for you? A tailored suit is not only guaranteed to be beautifully put together, but will be made for you and you alone, taking all your physical quirks and peculiarities into account.

Best for Ambience Spitalfield-style
Timothy Everest

32 Elder Street, E1. Tel (0171) 377 5770

Don't be put off by the Victorian edifice that houses this studio. Timothy Everest is a modern tailor that notoriously-hard-to-please fashion editors frequent. A former assistant of Tommy Nutter, he is a fairly recent arrival, but is professional to the last stitch. He has a ready-to-wear line and will make up a full suit for £725.

Best for Bespoke Fabrics
Richard James

31 Savile Row, W1. Tel (0171) 434 0605

If you have a dream fabric in mind, Richard James can accommodate you. With James's suits on their backs, cut from camouflage material, East 17 recently danced and sang their way through a range of public appearances. Richard James made his name by putting the colour back into pinstripes and is responsible for the uniforms at trendy restaurants such as the Atlantic Bar and Grill, and Coast. Off-the-peg designs can be found at Liberty and, for up to £950, he will make you an unforgettable creation.

Best for Flamboyant Colours

Ozwald Boateng

9 Vigo Street, W1. Tel (0171) 734 6868

This successful tailor has a real flair for rich colours to complement his modern designs. Celebrities such as Lenny Henry and Tori Amos drape themselves in his clothes, as well as tourists and city gents. A suit costs about £1,200 to make, including the fabric, and Boateng calls his creations 'bespoke couture'.

Best for Pampering Without Pretension

Mark Powell Bespoke Tailoring

17 Newburgh Street, W1. Tel (0171) 287 5498

In the 1980s, Mark Powell used to work from his fashionable Soho premises, but he has now shut up shop and works to appointment only. He has a ready-to-wear line or can knock up something in a week from £650–£950. He has an array of fashionable high-profile clients, including Naomi Campbell and George Michael. Should a man want a catsuit made to measure, Mark will not bat an eyelid!

Best for Spotting Rogue Actors and Rebel Rock Stars

John Pearse

6 Meard Street, W1. Tel (0171) 434 0738

The price-tag may be expensive but, at John Pearse, you are paying for experience. This is alternative tailoring at its best and the likes of Jack Nicholson, Dennis Hopper and Mick Jagger flock here. John Pearse has a collection of 'stand-out-in-the-crowd' ties and shirts, and wild-design suits. Prices for an off-the-peg suit start at £400 and a bespoke suit £700.

Tailor-made Shirts

Plucking your fashion-statement shirt from a local department store is rather like shopping for food. It looks all right on the packaging, but you don't really know whether it will live up to its promise. A shirtmaker, on the other hand, gives you the kind of personal service and the kind of shirt that keeps you coming back for more.

Best for Friendly Service
Hilditch & Key

73 Jermyn Street, SW1. Tel (0171) 930 5336

Sale-time is an excellent time to come here – the staff are supremely friendly, and you can feel comfortable browsing. A ready-made shirt costs around £60, or you can pay £115 for one made-to-measure. The process takes six weeks for the first shirt to be made, but, since your order must consist of at least six, expect to wait another six weeks before you can actually take them home. Worth the wait!

Best for Military Types
Stephan Haroutunian Shirts

95 Moore Park Road, SW6. Tel (0171) 731 5008

This family-owned business started in Cyprus in 1928 and moved to London in the 1960s. They are the official shirtmakers to a number of regiments and have a broad client list which includes members of parliament and visiting dignitaries. They will make you a shirt to measure for £43 and you can buy a ready-made one for £29.50. The atmosphere is efficient and the staff are very helpful.

Best for Mail Order
Foley and Foley

Unit 1, 1A Philip Walk, SE15. Tel (0171) 639 4807

Stephen Foley used to work in Jermyn Street, but now promises to make you a mail-order shirt within four weeks. A made-to-measure poplin shirt costs £52.50 and a ready-to-wear shirt costs £36.50.

Best for Star Customers
Turnbull & Asser

23 Berry Street, SW1. Tel (0171) 930 0502

If you are a first-time buyer who wants a shirt made especially for you, then you will need to buy six. From between £100 and £155, shirts like these could prove to be an investment! You will find yourself rubbing shoulders with royalty, models and film actresses. Worn-out collars and cuffs can be replaced for £25, and a ready-made shirt can be bought for £65.

Best for Variety
Thomas Pink

2 Donovan Court, Drayton Gardens, SW10. Tel (0171) 373 5795

They don't actually make shirts here, but there's such a wide variety of patterns, collar sizes and arm lengths to choose from that you are bound to find one that could have been made for you. The staff are on hand to help you find your way through the mountains of shirts adorning the shelves. Shirts costs from £35; they also sell ties, socks and cufflinks.

Tattooists

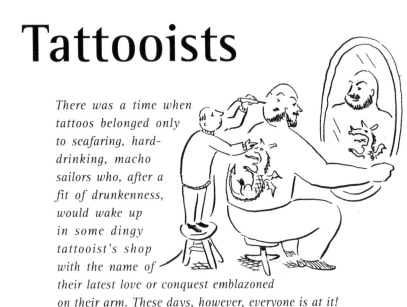

There was a time when tattoos belonged only to seafaring, hard-drinking, macho sailors who, after a fit of drunkenness, would wake up in some dingy tattooist's shop with the name of their latest love or conquest emblazoned on their arm. These days, however, everyone is at it!

Best General All-rounder

George Bone

58 Boston Road, W7. Tel (0181) 579 0831

George Bone has been a tattooist for 32 years. His most popular requests are for Japanese Work consisting of Samurai Warriors, dragons, etc., Western Work consisting of Confederate flags and what-nots, and Tribal, which is mostly abstract symbols. For the young, his most popular tattoos are Celtic New-Age. He never states a price until he has seen the individual and assessed what is wanted. A small tattoo takes 30 minutes, others can take up to eight hours.

Best Removal by Laser

Lasercare

144 Harley Street, W1. Tel (0171) 224 0988

Lasering is a gradual process which works by dispersing the particles of ink. Eventually, there should be no scars left or any lasting alteration to skin pigmentation. Tattoos have even been removed from people's genitals. It can take up to 15 sessions at £85 per session, but an upper price limit can be negotiated for a large area/number of tattoos. For the unemployed, who feel that their tattoos are jeopardising their search for a job, free work can be arranged.

Best Removal by Surgery

Bryan Mayou

The Lister Hospital, Chelsea Bridge Hospital, SW1. Tel (0171) 740 3417

So you've made a mistake or you're just sick of the sight of the damn thing. Bryan Mayou, a consultant at the Lister Hospital, will relieve you of the problem by surgically removing the tattoo, leaving newer, albeit scarred, tissue underneath. Costs from £500 to £1,000.

Best for Transfers

The Garage

350 Kings Road, SW3. Tel (0171) 351 3504

If you know your mother and father wouldn't like it or you just don't feel ready for a total commitment, why not go the way of the Super-models who recently attended the Catwalks of Paris and Milan sporting transfers that look just like real tattoos? There are many varieties to choose from and they look realistic enough to give your parents a heart attack. It's cheap too at £4.95 for a sheet of ten.

Best for Trendy Tattoos

Skinflash

Kensington Market, W8. Tel (0171) 937 2861

Andy Dixon of Skinflash says that there is no tattoo that he will not do. Roses and butterflies are standard favourites but he is willing to try anything. The smallest tattoo will set you back around £25, rising to £5,000 for a full back, chest and rib-cage job. Sessions can take from two minutes to 15 hours.

Tennis Coaching

During the end of June and the first week of July 'ordinary' tennis players used to brush the dust from their racquets and start to play in honour of the Wimbledon Tennis Championships. Now, however, instead of this passionate two-week fling with the sport, people are opting for a more prolonged and dedicated approach.

Best for a Beautiful Setting

Holland Park (Royal Borough of Kensington and Chelsea)

Booking Office, Stable Yard, Ilchester Place, W8. Tel (0171) 602 2226

Holland Park has six courts with balls provided, and a £1 charge for renting a racquet. There are three LTA-licensed coaches. A six-week two-hour group lesson costs £57 for adults; £26 for juniors.

Best for Incredible Coaching

Battersea Park Tennis Courts (Borough Of Wandsworth)

Battersea Park, SW11. Tel (0181) 871 7542

Highly-qualified coaches teach you volleys and back-hands over 23 hard courts and ten flood-lit courts. Private lessons for adults cost £23 per hour, plus a court fee. Before 6pm, the court fee is £3.50; after 6pm, £4. A registration card costs £9.

Best for Proximity to Wimbledon

Wimbledon Park (Borough Of Merton)

Home Park Road, SW19. Tel (0181) 879 0611

There are three LTA-licensed coaches at Wimbledon Park to teach you on ten hard courts and ten Astroturf courts. An annual membership of £10 enables you to use all the facilities. There are after-school courses, courses for the over-50s, and women-only classes. A one-hour private adult class costs £18.50, while an eight-week course of one-hour classes costs £32 for members and £36 for non-members.

Best for Wide-reaching Classes

Bishop's Park (Borough Of Hammersmith and Fulham)

Bishop's Avenue, SW6. Tel (0171) 736 3854

Classes here cater for everyone and there are 15 courts which are resurfaced every two to three years. There are four LTA-licensed full-time coaches, plus freelance coaches who are subject to regular background checks. For adults, a six-week course of one-hour group lessons costs £30. The weekend course is £40. They also have junior courses, coaching for the over-50s and the unemployed, and wheelchair tennis.

Best for Young Tennis

Rocks Lane Tennis Centre (Borough Of Richmond)

Rocks Lane, SW13. Tel (0181) 876 8330

One of the four LTA-licensed coaches here specialises in coaching young children. There are tournaments for juniors, mini tennis, short tennis, and youngsters can even enter the draw for Wimbledon tickets. Children from six to 18 years who are keen to brush up their skills can take part in a subsidised squad for only £3.50 an hour. A private lesson for adults or children costs £17 an hour, plus a court fee of £3.20 peak time, or £2.80 other times. A weekend intensive costs £36.

Toyshops

Big kids (fathers who have never grown up!) and small kids can spend hours amusing themselves in toyshops. The spectacle of little kids watching in stunned silence as their fathers take over the train sets and racing car controls is not uncommon. Toyshops are another world in which the young can try to be themselves while their parents regress.

Best for Another World
Harrods
87-135 Brompton Road, SW1. Tel (0171) 730 1234

Whether you're young or old, you can't fail to enjoy this toy department. It really is a chance to step into another world, to lose yourself among the cuddly toys or stand and play at the Dunlop pool. It's the misty-eyed adults who have to be dragged away - usually by children eager to crown the occasion with an ice-cream downstairs.

Best for Consumer Kids
Disney Store
140 Regent Street, W1. Tel (0171) 287 6558

Pocahontas is the name on the lips of every small child and, since children are consumer-mad with no money-worries, they are determined to have her. In this store, everything – dolls, cuddly toys, plates, cups, and caps - is within children's reach. No wonder there are tears before bedtime and so many kids having tantrums!

Best for Detail
Childsplay
112 Tooting High Street, SW17. Tel (0181) 672 6470

The first thing most children do is undress their dolls only to find that there are no gender differences at all. The only way they can be sure that Action Man is the real thing is by his haircut and army fatigues. At Childsplay, however, there are ways of telling a male from a female doll. An education in every sense of the word!

Best for Dream Houses

Never Land

3 Midhurst Parade, Fortis Green, N10. Tel (0181) 883 3997

Buy the house of your dreams in the form of a dolls' house, which come in kits from £25 upwards. You can either do it the cheap way – furnishing it with plastic children can play with; or the expensive way – with antiques, which could lead you to spend more on the toy than the real thing!

Best for Early Education

Early Learning Centre

160-161 Kensington High Street, W8. Tel (0171) 937 0419

Children can play happily here while parents decide if and what to buy. There is a variety of child-proof toys which have become firm favourites. The kids can play house with the cooker inside the shop or take a ride in a sturdy plastic car outside. Not all toys are big and expensive - there is a wide range for under £5.

Trips and Tours

Walking aimlessly past London's famous landmarks on your way to work each morning doesn't mean you know any more about them than your average Japanese tourist. Who hasn't heard Londoners behind them on the bus mixing up their monuments? So consult the experts and learn a bit more about your surroundings – even down to who lies six feet under at Highgate cemetary.

Best for Famous People From the Past

Highgate Cemetry

Swain's Lane, N6. Tel (0181) 340 1834

Graveyards can be both spooky and romantic places. Here at Highgate on selected Sundays, you can wander alone through the cemetery, past the catacombs and tombs. For those searching for the famous there is a suggested fee of £3 for one of the guided tours. No one has time to read the inscription on every stone and with an expert to guide you, you can be at Karl Marx's grave, rather than Joe Bloggs's, in minutes.

Best for Football Fanatics

Wembley Stadium Tour

Tel (0181) 902 8833

If you haven't watched a football match here then you might have watched a pop concert. This popular venue has been open since 1923 and is the home of the England football team. The tour includes a visit to the royal box and the dressing rooms and the chance to walk through the player's tunnel to the rather tinny sound of a crowd's applause. Every young boy dreams of the day when they will play for their country and run out on to the pitch, so this tour is sure to bring a smile to the faces of both small and big kids alike.

Best for Guiding You Back Through Time

Dennis Severs House

18 Folgate Street, E1. Tel (0171) 247 4013

For £30 you can turn back the clock, forget the trappings of modern times and appreciate the simplicity of days gone by. Dennis Severs has recreated a little of eighteenth- and nineteenth-century London in his own house. Each room is decorated in the style of a different era and the attention to the smallest details has produced a real ambience without any tacky gimmicks. Severs has even created an imaginary family whose fortunes you can follow through the centuries as the tour progresses. Visitors are requested to bring their imaginations with them if they attend one of the three tours conducted here each week.

Best London Guide

William Forrester

1 Belvedere Road, Guildford, Surrey. Tel (01483) 575401

For a highly amusing and informative trip around London, William Forrester is your man. He leaves no stone unturned and pays special attention to every detail. His illustrated guides and talks are totally fascinating; you won't find yourself yawning or clockwatching in his presence. Forrester himself is a wheelchair user and takes disabled as well as able-bodied people on his tours. You are guaranteed a good time; the only drawback is that you have to book your trip well in advance.

Tutorials

If your child is a bit of a rebel, and has failed his or her A-Levels first time round, or just can't settle down at school, a tutorial college might be the best solution. These colleges are there to get results and are a popular option for wayward children.

Best for All-round Attention

Davies, Land & Dick

10 Pembridge Square, W2. Tel (0171) 727 2797

At Davies, Land & Dick, all pupils, regardless of their capabilities, are encouraged and a much struggled-for E grade is considered just as impressive as an A grade. The emphasis is on nurturing individual talents and this is reflected in the wide-ranging curriculum, which includes film-making and word-processing. Prices are from £2,600 a term.

Best for Art

Fine Art College

85 Belsize Park Gardens, NW3. Tel (0171) 586 0312

The Fine Art College is considered to be the next stage after school, but before a student reaches university level. The school itself is very small and accepts students from all around the world. The teaching staff are personable and classes are innovative and very well-taught. Various sports, visits to the theatre and trips abroad are just some of the many extra-curricular activities. Prices are from £2,195 a term.

Best for Being on Your Case

Mander, Portman & Woodward

108 Cromwell Road, SW7; and 24 Elvaston Place, SW1. Tel (0171) 835 1355

Most pupils here are ex-public school children retaking exams or those who need a change from the normal school atmosphere. The emphasis is on the individual and class numbers are small. Personal tutors monitor your offspring and spend most of the week on the phone to you or to universities in order to give progress reports. Fees are £2,337 a term for three A-Level subjects over two years.

Best for the Budding Scientist

Abbey International College

28A Hereford Road, W2. Tel (0171) 229 5928

This no-nonsense school deals specifically with the sciences, maths and economics, and directs A-Level students into university courses such as medicine, dentistry, pharmacy and law. It does not use personal tutors or have extra-curricular activities; the time is spent going over past exam papers – simple, no-nonsense hard work. Prices are from £1,900 per term.

Best for Making the Grade

Ashbourne Tutors

17 Old Court Place, W8. Tel (0171) 937 3858

This college will make cynics of such establishments eat their words. They are highly successful at obtaining much-needed grades and school work is attacked with great vigour, with students constantly being tested. The atmosphere is relaxed but determined, and the students are expected to work as hard as they play. Extra-curricular activities are wide and varied. Prices are from £2,650 a term.

Twenty-four-hour Shops

People are always complaining that there is never enough time to fit everything they need to do into a day. Fortunately, there are now a collection of obliging people who keep their doors open 24 hours a day to satisfy their frenetic customers.

Best All-night Munchies
Vingt Quatre

325 Fulham Road, SW10. Tel (0171) 376 7224

Oliver Vigors, Joel Cadbury, and Alex Langland Pierce bought and turned around this rather seedy 'Up all Night' to add to their other ventures along the Fulham Road – The Goat in Boots and The King's Club. 'Everything is quality here,' says Oliver Vigors and they keep all their customers – from the smart Chelsea set to hospital workers at the Chelsea & Westminster – happy. The décor is modern, bright and funky, and this is definitely a place to see and be seen in. The menu – from £1.50 to £9.50 – is varied and extremely reasonably priced. You can have anything from a bowl of cereal, to bangers-and-mash, and duck. This place is well worth a visit.

Best for Convenience
7-Eleven (selected branches):

Hammersmith, 134 King Street, W6. Tel (0181) 846 9154
South Kensington, 119 Gloucester Road, SW7. Tel (0171) 373 1440

This American chain, filled to the brim with essential night-time snacks, is definitely worth a visit as you drag yourself home after work or when you are out and about in the middle of the night. One thing you have to remember when you come here is to make a visit to a cash dispenser – 7-Eleven is notoriously expensive.

Best for Coping with Fido
Emergency Veterinary Clinic

55 Elizabeth Street, SW1. Tel (0171) 730 9102

Unfortunately, neither people nor animals can control the hours when they feel ill or have an accident. People have the round-the-clock service of a hospital (if they're prepared to wait!) and animals now have an ambulance service and an operating theatre. There is no NHS for animals, however, and, while during the day the prices here are comparable with vets, the cost rises at night.

Best for Cruising
The Wonder Years

264 Merton Road, SW18. Tel (0181) 871 2777

London looks best by night, especially when you are cruising around in style, feeling like a movie star, in a chauffeur-driven Bentley. If a Bentley does not suit you, maybe a Rolls Royce or a stretch Cadillac with tinted windows will. The only snag is that you have to hire the car for a minimum of four hours. How many times can you go round London in that time?

Best for Snappers
Joe's Basement

113 Wardour Street, W1. Tel (0171) 434 9313
83-88 Clerkenwell Road, EC1. Tel (0171) 253 6000

If you ever need your photographs in a rush and cannot wait for the one-hour shop to open in the morning, Joe's Basement is the place to go. This professional photographic laboratory will process a 24-exposure film for £4.50, plus VAT, and 36-exposure films for £7 plus VAT. If you can wait 24 hours, a 36-exposure film costs the same as a 24-exposure.

Vets

Polly is as sick as the proverbial, and Dan-the-dog's temperature is soaring. Where do you take your poorly pet? Usually it's a question of looking for the nearest local vet, but it's best to find out a few facts first. Listed below are just some of London's best-known vets.

Best Bookish Vet

Bruce Fogle

The Portman Veterinary Clinic, 86 York Street, W1. Tel (0171) 723 2068

Canadian Bruce Fogle is well known everywhere in the animal world for his informative books on dogs, including 'Questions Your Dog Would Ask If Your Dog Could Talk'. Popular in central London, his surgery is much enhanced by his two resident Boxer dogs.

Best Charitable Vet

The Blue Cross Animal Hospital

1, Hugh Street, SW1. Tel (0171) 834 4224/(0171) 834 5556

A really excellent organisation, this charity has been running since 1897 and its Victoria branch alone treats more than 27,000 cases a year. In order for their pet to qualify for treatment, pet-owners have to be in receipt of State benefits and are then asked to donate whatever they can afford. Some operations, for example, cost the charity hundreds of pounds and it may only receive £1 or less in return. There is a 24-hour emergency service. There are two other London branches at Hammersmith and Wandsworth. Ring the main switchboard above for details.

Best for Heart Conditions

Andrew Carmichael

Addison Veterinary Clinic, 7 Addison Avenue, W11. Tel (0171) 603 4407

Known as the Christian Barnard of the animal world, vets from all over London refer their clients to this practice if the animal is suffering from a dodgy ticker. This practice also specialises in exotic animals, including parrots and reptiles. Open: Monday to Saturday, 9am–11am and 4.30pm–6.30pm. (Wednesday, 4.30pm–6pm; Thursday 4.30pm–7pm). Standard consultation fee is £22, plus VAT.

Best-looking Vet

Christian Fabricius

535 Battersea Park Road, SW11. Tel (0171) 924 5350)

This state-of-the-art vet works from his state-of-the-art surgery in Battersea. He has a huge following of ladies, and his patients are fiercely loyal. He will do home-visits and his surgery has an up-beat atmosphere. Open: Monday to Friday, 9am–11am and 4pm–6pm, (Monday and Thursday, to 7pm); surgery Saturday, 9am–11am. Standard consultation fee is £13 including VAT.

Best for the Royal Borough

Keith Butt

Kynance Veterinary Clinic, 8 Kynance Mews, SW7. Tel (0171) 584 2019)

Ask anyone in Kensington and Chelsea, from debs to dowagers, where they take their pet and the name Keith Butt will spring up. Even though his clients are some of the most demanding in London Keith Butt is as well known for his charm, which is legendary in the Royal Borough, as for his veterinary skills. Good all-rounder. Open: Monday to Thursday, 8am. to 5.30pm; Friday, 8am. to 5pm. Standard consultation fee £20, plus VAT.

Video Shops

It's dark, it's late, everything seems to have closed down, and your favourite choc-ice is beckoning from the fridge. What better companion than a video to ward off those lonely blues or enhance that couple feeling? Or maybe you are just fed up with your job, have got the 'flu or just want to stay in bed for the day. There is no better feeling than having rung up the boss and excused yourself for the day then snuggling down with some celluloid. Nowadays films are barely off the cinema screens before they are looming large in your sitting room.

Best All-rounder

Video City

117 Notting Hill Gate, W11. Tel (0171) 221 7029

This little shop has become something of an institution for the local hill-billy population. Established 15 years ago, Video City is one of the oldest and most respected video outlets in London. The staff are always willing to give advice, and the range is truly vast. Rental cost: every day except Wednesday, £3 per night; Wednesday, £1 per night. Twenty-three per cent discount for UB40 holders. Opening hours: Sunday to Thursday, 9am–10.30pm; Friday and Saturday, 9am–midnight, Sundays 12am–9pm.

Best for Arty Farties

Vultures Videos

1 Goldhurst Terrace, NW6. Tel (0171) 372 7476 and 133 Upper Street, N1

This emporium has just about everything you could ever dream of. There are about 4,500 titles of which 300 are billed as modern classics from all over the world. This is a 'happening' place where a visit is likely to turn into a social event. The staff will reserve or purchase any film on request. Rental cost: new releases £2.50 per night; old releases £2.00; children's 50p–£1.00. Open seven days a week.

Best for those Late-night Munchies

Flicks Video

622 Fulham Road, SW6. Tel (0171) 731 7350

One of a chain of five, Flicks Video is a small local shop with a vast range of over 3,000 titles in stock and a huge array of pic'n'mix sweets and ice-creams to satsify those late-night munchies as you snuggle down to the film of your choice. It also has a good range of ex-rental films for sale at a reasonable price. There is an annual membership fee of £3. Rental cost: new releases, £2.50 per night/weekend; old releases, £1.50 to £2 per night; children's, £1 per night. Opening hours: daily, 11am–10pm. Mail slot for returns (24 hours).

Best for Up-to-the-Minute Blockbusters

Unit 5

The Junction Shopping Centre, SW11. Tel (0171) 738 2212

This is the largest Blockbuster branch in London and carries more than 10,000 titles with up to 100 copies of each film. Sidelines are wide-ranging, with a vast selection of goodies ranging from T-shirts, sweets, computer games; there is even a video player rental section. This place is really excellent for kids. Rental cost: new releases, £2.99 per night; older releases, £2.99 for three nights; children's, 99p per night. Opening hours: Sunday to Thursday, 9am–11pm, Friday and Saturday from 9am to midnight. Mail slot for returns (24 hours).

Wedding Dresses

Some brides-to-be dream of a classic white dress in which they glide radiantly down the aisle; others want to be adorned in all the colours of the rainbow. The good news is that, in London, all tastes can be catered for.

Best Alternative
Idol 15

Inglestre Place, W1. Tel (0171) 439 8537

Silk chiffon and velvet dresses are all the rage for those who are in search of something just a bit different. The dresses have Empire lines (perfect for shotgun weddings!) and come in three different styles. The beauty of these dresses is that they really can be worn time and time again; Idol will dye any dress to the colour and shade of your choice once the big day is over. Dresses cost from £300 to £1,000. If you want one made to measure, add an extra ten per cent.

Best Dressmaker
Fiona Clare

57 Queenstown Road, SW8. Tel (0171) 978 5728

Fiona Clare will create your dream dress without ever telling you what you should wear. Fiona spends her time coming up with new and wonderful ideas. Her dresses have a historical feel and she makes a variety of boned-and-beaded corsets. Four-to-six fittings later, you will have a gorgeous gown costing from £1,500.

Best Newcomer

Trudy Hanson

Studio 21, Buspace Studios, Conlan Street, W10. Tel (0181) 964 9390

These beautiful, simple dresses have a movie-star elegance about them. Hanson, who makes beautiful period designs, has just moved into the ready-to-wear market. She excels in embroidery and will take three-to-five fittings to deliver a masterpiece. Her dresses cost from £800 to £3,300.

Best for Second-hand

The Wedding Dress Exchange

97 Claxton Grove, W6. Tel (0171) 788 2181

Spending huge sums of money on a dress that will be worn for only a couple of hours, can seem total madness for the thrifty among us. At this shop, however, you can pick up a designer dress for a fraction of its original cost and no one will be any the wiser. Owner Mary Nicholson has dresses in stock from David Fielden and Bruce Oldfield. They are sold for half their original price and the owner is given 60 per cent. Prices are from £90 to £3,450.

Best for Traditional Lines

Phillipa Lepley

494 Fulham Road, SW6. Tel (0171) 386 0927

Phillipa Lepley's creations are best described as classic and the finished product is bound to please both bride and stressed mother. The dresses are designed to show a girl's figure to its best advantage, particularly the waist. Designs are not fussy and concentrate on detail around the neck and hem lines. If you want to show off the family tiara without over-shadowing the dress, Phillipa makes a simple V-front panelled bodice which will complement it perfectly. Prices start from £2,500.

Wedding Lists

Inviting 100 people to your wedding and expecting them not to duplicate presents is rather unrealistic. You could ask them on the invitation to bring a certain item, like a Cartier trinket or a cheque for £1,000 (and come off it, we all know that's what we'd really like), but that would be considered rude. Personally, I think we should take a leaf out of the Greek Orthodox book of weddings, and get our guests to pin hard currency on to the bride's wedding dress. The most realistic solution, to avoid 100 toasters and to guarantee a present that you want, is to set up a wedding list.

Best for Efficiency

General Trading Company

144 Sloane Street, SW1. Tel (0171) 730 0411

The bride is given ten per cent credit to the value of gifts bought for her at GTC, along with a leather-bound photo album. So, it is a wise move to ensure that none of your guests strays and buys things elsewhere. Presents can either be ordered by phone or in person and a copy of the list will be sent on request. The bride-to-be will be notified on the day a gift is purchased.

Best for Exclusive Gifts

Wedding List Services

44 Gowrie Road, SW11. Tel (0171) 978 1118

There is no fee involved here and brides make up their list from showroom samples, such as wine from Berry Bros & Rudd and linens from the White Company. Wedding List Services keeps hold of the list and guests can buy their presents over the phone with a credit card. Weekly updates on what has been purchased are made and sent to the bride-to-be. Presents are wrapped and delivered for no extra cost.

Best No-frills Service

Peter Jones

Sloane Square, SW1. Tel (0171) 730 0200

Guests can order in person or over the phone in the Storewide Bride's Book Service. Presents can be delivered with the purchaser's name. The Bride will receive a summary, just before her big day, of all that has been bought.

Best for Out-of-Town Guests

Marks & Spencer

P.O Box 288, Warrington, Cheshire. Tel (01925) 812 525

If you have invited some out-of-towners to your wedding, they can still buy you something from your list with the help of M&S's wedding service. A card can be sent showing where the list is available nation-wide or they can telephone an order. The list of who bought what can be supplied after the wedding. There is a small fee for wrapping and delivery.

Best for Personal Services

The Wedding List Company

91 Walton Street, SW3. Tel (0171) 584 1222

Here, the bride-to-be is not restricted to what is available in the shop, but given a catalogue to peruse and choose from. Lists can be sent to guests, but they can also call the shop and discuss items. The shop has cards engraved to show where the list is being held and has weekly updates on who has bought what. The cost is £75 and they will wrap the presents purchased for a further small fee.

Wigs

Today's wigs are so realistic, they can look like your own hair. They are fabulous for allowing a little versatility in how you choose to look. Whether you have short or long hair, you can change your image whenever you feel like it.

Best for Extensions
Harrods Hair and Beauty Salon

5th floor, Harrods, Knightsbridge, SW1. Tel (0171) 730 1234

Do you fancy long hair but are frustrated because yours only just brushes your ears? Then how about a hair extension? At Harrods, they will weave five or six different shades of hair into your own mop to achieve a natural look. It takes up to five or six hours to complete and is quite costly at £80 an hour. It all depends on how badly you want to change your image!

Best for Hairpieces
Trendco

229 Kensington Church Street, W8. Tel (0171) 221 2646

Whether you are looking for a hairpiece to give you extra 'oomph' or simply to cover your bald spot, this is the place to come. You can also have a custom-made piece, made from human hair, for an invisible match. The staff advise you to take time for a consultation – there is nothing more toe-curlingly awful than a man with a bad-fitting hairpiece. The price of an average wig is about £80.

Best for Party Wigs
Angels & Bermans

119 Shaftesbury Avenue, WC2. Tel (0171) 836 5678

It is not just heads that are catered for at this fancy-dress shop – chests, too can be covered in lustrous locks of hair. None of the wigs here would win prizes for reality, but they are sufficiently over the top for a fancy-dress party. You could give the Beatles' revival a boost by sporting a fab-four mop, or try the Ann Hathaway for £15.

Best for Serious Wigs

Hair Raisers

105 Cleveland Street, W1. Tel (0171) 580 7666

With more than 600 wigs to choose from, you are bound to find something to suit you at Hair Raisers. There are wigs on sale in 20 different colours and it is possible to buy one which costs less than the average haircut. Wigs available include the high-altitude kind, with curls piled up to dizzy heights on the head, as well as more compact, frosted and teased ones.

Index

Index